MW00577560

BUTTERFLIES & LEMONADE

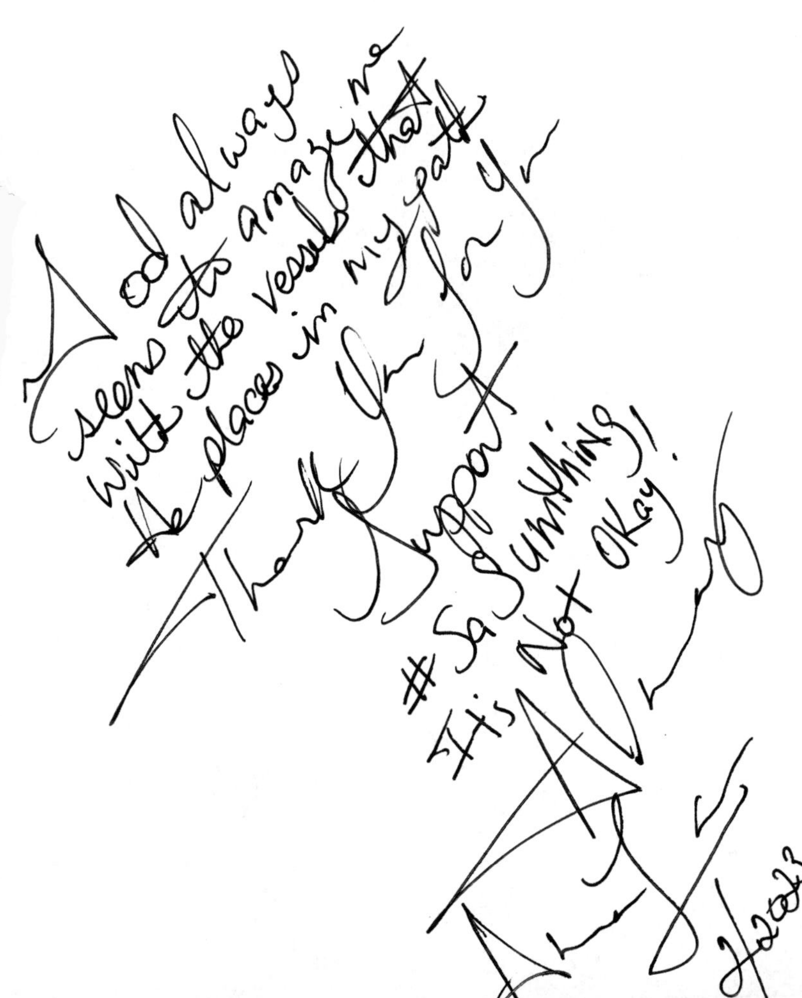

Butterflies & Lemonade

Summer Heat

A DIVINE JOURNEY
Atlanta, Georgia

A DIVINE JOURNEY
An imprint of Grace Royal International LLC
graceroyal-intl.com

Published in the United States of America by A Divine Journey, an imprint and division of Grace Royal International LLC, Atlanta, GA.
For additional information, including bulk shipping options, address Grace Royal International electronically at Publisher@graceroyal-intl.com.

Atlanta, GA
Subject: Biographical Fiction

Hardcover ISBN: 978-0-578-96894-0
Paperback ISBN: 979-8-485-09166-8
Ebook ISBN: 978-0-578-96895-7

PRINTED IN THE UNITED STATES OF AMERICA

For Ari & Jasmine

This book is dedicated to my daughter, Ariona Porter, and my niece, Jasmine Parker, who have persevered and prospered while fighting battles most knew nothing of.

#SaSumthing

Chapter One

Mama

"For I know the plans I have for you,"
declares the Lord, "plans to prosper you and not
to harm you, plans to give you hope and a future."
-Jeremiah 29:11

"Here go mama's braid!" I shouted up to my eldest sister as she plaited what was left of Mama's hair. Sometimes, Mama's whole braid would fall off while Reign was plaiting it. She was sick and as far as my five-year-old brain knew, that's what happened when you were sick.

Reign took the braid out of my tiny palm and studied it. "Go put it in the box," she told me as she handed it back. I looked up at Mama sitting in bed and hooked up to her oxygen tank. She said nothing. She stared past me towards the small TV in the room. She was distant. I didn't know if she was ignoring me, or simply did not want another reminder of what was happening to her.

I got up from the bed and followed my sister's directions. There were four other large plaits already in the box. I stared at them for a while, placed the new one in the box and closed it. I looked over at my sister and Mama and took in their silence. I knew something was wrong, but I couldn't understand it.

Mama and I had a special relationship. I never went to daycare or preschool. Mama was too sick to work, so she stayed home with me. In some ways, Mama and I just took care of each other.

Mama had good days and bad days. There were the good days that I would watch her get dressed and we would drive to the hospital for her appointments and the bad days where the appointments had to come to us.

On the good days, I would watch Mama stuff her bra with cotton as she got dressed. I really didn't understand what breast cancer was, so this became a norm for me. When I would play in her clothes, I would put on her bras and stuff them with cotton too.

When we went to the hospital, I was never allowed in the room with Mama, so the nurses would always find a way to keep me busy. They would give me a needleless syringe that I could fill with water and squirt across the room. Then, after each visit, I would take the syringe home and give my big sisters hell.

On the bad days, when the appointments had to come to us, I remember slipping the house key through a small hole in the screen door to let the medics in.

This was my norm. I learned how to keep myself busy. When we were at home, Mama let me do whatever I wanted. I would run around the house and go through my sisters' things while they were at school. Despite Mama being sick, I was just a happy, carefree kid.

I don't remember much before five. Everyone felt so much older than me that I can only remember feeling small. I felt invisible and invincible all at the same time. Because I did whatever I wanted, whenever I wanted, I could always count on Mama to keep me out of trouble when I got under Daddy's skin.

The closest sister in age to me was eight years older. Autumn. She was the docile one of the bunch and I gave her hell. I can remember slapping her with a hairbrush across the back one day just because she made me mad. She would never hit me back. She just wasn't a fan of drama or chaos. She was one to stay under the radar by following the rules.

My eldest sister, Daisy Reign, was attending an all girls college. She sold candy to keep herself afloat while my parents put my other sisters, Stormi and Autumn, through Catholic school. Whenever Reign was at school, I would go into her room and eat the candy she bought to sell on campus. I was that little sister.

Even though I did my best to keep myself busy throughout the day, I was always excited for my sisters to come home. I loved my Mama, but I was five... I needed my sisters.

When my sisters would come home, we would gather in Mama's room to get a run down of everyone's day. Mama was big on family meetings, family dinners, and family time. She did not grow up in a family of her own and wanted to create the supportive family unit she needed as a little girl.

When we would have these family discussions, Autumn was always the quiet one. She never shared much because she just didn't do much. Stormi, the second oldest, would stand strategically in the doorway avoiding Mama's gaze. She would attempt to be quiet like Autumn, but it would never last long. Reign, the oldest, would talk about college life, running track and selling candy on campus. I loved hearing Reign's stories. I would even follow her around when she was on the telephone talking to her boyfriend so I could gather some news to spread during our meetings.

Stormi was the one who stayed in trouble. She showed her ass at school. The school would call Mama well before she got home and Mama was always ready for her. Stormi was known at school for cussin' out the other kids, fighting the nuns, walking out of class, you name it. When she would get home to tell Mama about her day, she would attempt to concoct a whole new story and slither her way out of the room into the hallway. In hindsight, she probably should have been kicked out of that school. But, everyone at the school knew how sick Mama was and let things slide.

I remember the night Mama was so pissed off at Stormi's behavior that she sat up in the bed and asked one of us to hand her something. I handed her a glass of red juice that was close by. Mama took that glass and threw it right at Stormi. Stormi somehow managed to dodge the glass, but Mama still made her clean up the juice and broken glass that hit the floor.

Despite Stormi's behavior, Mama loved the four of us with everything she had and wanted the absolute best for us. She named us for the seasons in which we were born as a reminder that every thing had its season, its time, and its purpose on earth. Since I was born on the hottest day of July in 1972, she named me Summer Heat.

Those family meetings are among my favorite childhood memories of me, my Mama and my sisters. We were a perfectly imperfect family and I felt so loved and protected in their presence. It was during these meetings that Mama, knowing that she may never live to see it, would say, "Reign, I'm so proud of you. Stormi, Autumn, Heat, I want y'all to make sure to do one thing for me. Get your high school diploma."

Chapter Two

Cash

Take no part in the worthless deeds of evil and darkness; instead, expose them. It is shameful even to talk about the things that ungodly people do in secret. But their evil intentions will be exposed when the light shines on them, for the light makes everything visible.

-Ephesians 5: 11-14

I was motivated to finish high school because it was what Mama wanted. I just never knew the journey would be so... eventful. Mama and I were a lot alike. Even at a young age I admired her quick wit and straightforward demeanor. I remember riding in the car with her one night when things weren't going well with her and my dad. Mama pulled up next to my dad's girlfriend's car and wrote all over it with white shoe polish. All I remember thinking was, "Ooooooh daddy pissed Mama off!"

That incident would become a turning point in my parent's relationship. The family unit I once knew had begun to unravel when Mama put daddy out. Daddy went to stay with his girlfriend and started picking me up on occasion to spend the night. My older sisters would never come. They were all mad with my dad for reasons I couldn't understand at the time.

~ ~ ~

"Summer Heat! You ready to go?" I heard Daddy yell from outside. "Yes!" I shouted back as I finished putting my shoes on. I looked over at Stormi. She was sitting in the kitchen tearing up her second bag of chips. She looked at me and rolled her eyes. She knew I would come back bragging about what I got to do with daddy.

I walked out of the front door and ran straight towards daddy's car. "Come on now Heat! I have to go pick up Queen and Cash!" Daddy fussed as I pulled myself up into the car and pulled the door closed. I looked back at the house as we pulled off. I thought of my sisters and their refusal to come. Maybe they were right about something, but I still struggled to understand what.

I rode in the backseat staring out of the window. After about ten minutes, we pulled up to a tall, white building. Daddy blew the horn twice and his girlfriend, Queen, walked out with her son directly behind.

"Hi Heat!" Queen stated as she opened daddy's passenger side door. "Hi Miss Queen!" I answered. Unlike my sisters, I never had a problem with Queen. She was always pleasant towards me and I grew to like her a lot. Queen's 9-year-old son Cash opened the passenger side back door and hopped in the back with me. He pushed my shoulder, "What's Up Heat! You staying with us tonight?" "Yep!" I said. "Cool." He replied and looked out the window.

After a thirty - minute ride, we pulled up at Queen's two-bedroom house. We entered through the kitchen and Cash walked straight towards the stairs to his room. My dad took my overnight bag and called him back, "Cash! Take Heat's bag upstairs to your room." Cash walked back towards my dad and grabbed the bag. He looked at me briefly and continued to his room with my bag.

"Heat, Queen and I are going out tonight."

"Can I come?"

"No, you and Cash will stay here. We only going to be out for a little bit."

"OK," I responded sadly. In my mind, I wanted to spend time with my daddy. Not Cash. But, I knew once my father had a plan for what he was about to do, that was it. He was going to do it.

Daddy and Queen left around 6 o'clock that evening and didn't get home until close to midnight. When they came home, Cash and I were still up sitting on the couch watching TV.

"Y'all should be sleep!" Queen said, surprised that we were still up.

"Y'all go on upstairs and get ready for bed. Heat you can sleep in Cash's room," Daddy said.

"OK," I said, feeling sleepy. I got up and walked upstairs with Cash. Cash opened the door to his room and I followed him in.

"OK, you lay down on this side and I'll lay down on this side," Cash instructed.

"OK. I gotta go put on my pajamas," I responded looking for my bag. I spotted my bag in the corner and looked through it for my pajamas. I pulled out my favorite pink nightgown and went out in the hallway to look for my daddy.

"Daddy can you help me put on my PJ's?" I asked when I saw him walking towards Queen's room. "Heat, you're almost 6 now. You're a big girl. You can do it." He responded. Disappointed, I walked to the bathroom and got myself ready for bed.

I returned to Cash's room and he had changed into his blue basketball pajamas and was already laying in bed. I laid down where Cash told me I could and faced the wall. I remember wishing that Queen had a daughter so I wouldn't have to sleep in the bed with a boy. My concern was only based on the fact that I was 5 and used to being around my older sisters. At the time, I had no idea how our parents' seemingly insignificant sleeping arrangements would affect the trajectory of my life.

As I lay there longing for my sisters, I heard Queen's voice in the hallway. I looked up in time to see her peek her head in the room. She looked at me, turned off the light, and closed the door in. As I lay in the bed next to Cash, I struggled to fall asleep. I was sleepy, but it was my first time sleeping over Queen and Cash's house. It felt weird. When I finally started to drift off, I heard Cash's voice.

"Heat. Heat." Cash whispered.

"What?" I responded.

"Give me your hand." I held my hand out

towards him confused as to why he wanted my hand. Cash took my hand and pulled it toward his penis. "Hold this," he said.

As I held his penis, he started to tell me different things to do. I followed his directions slightly confused on why he would want me to hold something he used the bathroom with. After a few minutes, Cash grunted. "ILL," I said and looked at Cash. "SHH!" He whispered and then laughed.

Not fully grasping what had just happened, I laughed too and wiped my hand on his shirt.

"Don't tell nobody. Your daddy gonna be mad at you," he said.

"OK," I responded nonchalantly and laid back down towards the wall.

~ ~ ~

It all happened so fast. I don't remember feeling afraid or even like Cash was doing something to me that would echo for the rest of my life. I guess in some ways, I just thought we were playing. Strangely enough, I still knew it was the part of my time at daddy's that I couldn't tell my sisters about. I already knew I could not tell my dad because I didn't want him to be upset with me like Cash said he would.

The way Cash would always remind me not to tell anyone made me feel like there was an exciting secret between us.

As time went on Cash's advances grew from asking me to hold his penis to rubbing his body against mine until he ejaculated. It wasn't long before, I got used to it. Every night that I stayed with my daddy at Queen's and was made to sleep in Cash's bed, I expected for us to "play night time." When I would return home to my Mama and sisters, I would always act like nothing happened.

Chapter Three

Queen

"So do not fear, for I am with you; do not be dismayed, for I am your God. I will strengthen you and help you; I will uphold you with my righteous right hand."
-Isaiah 41:10

I WAS 6 YEARS OLD WHEN MAMA PASSED. I don't remember a whole lot of people being hysterical. I just remember sitting on the floor of our living room and hearing someone say, "Heat isn't going" as if I wasn't sitting right there. There seemed to be a world of things happening and decisions being made around me, but no one talked to me about what was happening, or even asked if

I was okay for that matter.

"Hey Ms. Jackson, thanks for coming to watch Heat during the funeral. She's in there watching TV." I heard Reign say.

"Not a problem. You all are in my prayers."

Ms. Jackson walked into the living room. "Hey Heat! You hungry?"

"No Ma'am," I responded.

As she walked back towards the kitchen, I heard the front door close. My sisters had left. I turned back towards the TV, mad. I might have looked like I was watching TV, but I was paying attention to everything happening around me and trying to make sense of it all. Why was no one talking to me? Or, asking me how I felt and if I wanted to go? Everyone dressed up that morning and got ready for my mother's funeral as if she wasn't my mother too. It seemed like no one cared how I felt.

I didn't know what to think about my mother's death and was angry at being left out. I felt like everyone abandoned me all at one time. My mama, my sisters, my dad, there was no one I could talk to. I was so confused.

This was the first time I told myself that no one really cared about me. My earliest memory of the feelings of abandonment. Mama, my protector, was gone. I felt incredibly alone as

I listened to Ms. Jackson moving around the kitchen on the day of Mama's funeral. I hated the feeling and at that moment I pushed it down as far as I could.

A few days after the funeral, daddy announced that he would be moving back into the house with Queen and Cash to take care of me and my sisters. My sisters were pissed. It became obvious that there were parts of the story between daddy and Queen that I didn't know and they were furious at how bold he was.

Queen and Cash moved into our home one month after my Mama's funeral. By this time, Reign was married, Stormi was two sheets in the wind, and Autumn was in High School preparing for college. Because they were so much older than me, I felt alone with Daddy, Queen, and Cash. It was like my sisters were becoming my old family and Queen and Cash were my new family.

Cash ended up with his own room while Autumn and I shared a room. At first, Stormi and Reign would pop in and out to visit, but as time passed their visits decreased and the calls stopped. Their inconsistency played on the raw feelings I still struggled to process sitting in front of the TV the day of Mama's funeral. Again, I told myself, no one really cared about me.

~ ~ ~

"Ma, can I get some juice?" I asked Queen. WHAP! I could feel the sting of Autumn's hand to the back of my neck. Autumn never hit me. I was so shocked, I didn't even hit her back.

"She ain't your Mama, Heat!" She sneered. I could do nothing but stare back at her. I was trying to get used to my new life. I wanted to have the family unit back that my Mama created, but it felt impossible. Calling Queen "Ma" was the only way I knew how to bring it back. Queen never asked me to call her mom, but I thought it was the right thing to do. Queen provided the motherly nurturing I needed in my mother's absence so I didn't see the problem with calling her Ma. She had always been nice to me so, I had no personal reason to dislike her.

Low-key, everyone knew Queen was happy to move in. That townhouse she lived in was in the hood. I was excited to have a mother figure still in my life, even if my sister's hated it. Daddy worked 7 days a week for 12-14 hours a day as an electrician. In his absence, Queen would take me to school programs and down to Augusta to visit her family. When he was home, he was asleep, doing yard work or working on his cars. So, with daddy working nonstop and Mama being gone, Queen helped to fill the void of two missing parents. At that age, I didn't see her role as problematic. She took on the role of mother and I appreciated it.

Queen was always dressed in designer clothes and made sure we looked good too. Before Autumn went off to college, Queen would take me, Autumn, and Cash school shopping. We loved Rich's and Richway. With Queen's high taste for fashion and daddy's money, I always dressed well and looked good. But, despite Queen's best efforts, my older sister, Autumn, hated both Queen and Cash. When she finally went off to college, it was like she ran away and never looked back.

Chapter Four

Eleven Years Old

For nothing is hidden that will not be made manifest, nor is anything secret that will not be known and come to light.
-Luke 8:17

"WHAT YOU WATCHING?" CASH ASKED.

"Wheel of Fortune" I responded.

"This show is wack!" Cash stated as he poked me in the side. He always started with tickling me. I immediately knew how this would end.

I jumped and laughed, "Stop! No it's not!"

"Yes it is!" Cash laughed and started poking me again.

As I laughed and jumped, I felt his hands moving from poking to tickling to fondling.

Daddy and Queen had gone to a friends house to play cards for the evening. As usual, Cash and I were left at home alone to take care of each other.

As we laughed and played around in front of the TV, I felt Cash become erect. After 6 years, I had become used to this "game." I knew Cash would ask me to touch his penis next and I, thinking nothing more of it than a game, would oblige. I knew we would then fondle each other until we heard our parents return. "Don't say nothin'" he would always whisper right as Queen and my daddy would walk through the door. This was our norm. Our little secret.

After Autumn went off to college, Cash and I were often left home alone while daddy and Queen went out. Every time we were alone, Cash and I would "play around." By the time I was 11 years old and Cash was 15, I felt like we were in a secret relationship. That excited me and I developed a huge crush on him.

I imagined Cash being my boyfriend so often that when his real high school girlfriend started coming over, I would give her hell. I would pinch her when no one was looking and give her the silent treatment. I didn't fully understand why I was feeling the way I did or choosing to behave that way. I just knew that she was a threat to my made-up relationship with Cash and I didn't like her being around. In some ways, it felt like Cash was cheating on me.

~ ~ ~

"Get off of me!" Cash shouted as Autumn held him down on the living room floor.

"Wear his ass out!" Autumn would shout as I hit him over and over again.

Autumn used to come home from college on occasion and when she would come home, she would always want to fight Cash. I never told her what was going on, but it seemed like somehow she knew and this was her way at getting at him. I would wear Cash out like she said, but my mind was never really on Cash's advances. It was on the fact that he had girlfriend. This was the boy who took my innocence at five. How dare he like someone else?

The thing is, Cash was never aggressive with me, so I would have never seen him as an abuser. Cash was smart and even enrolled in a high achievers' math program in High School. It was not until years later I would realize the complete mental fog that I was going through as a result of this early sexual abuse. There was no way I could have known any of this was wrong or the lasting impact it would have on how I viewed my romantic relationships.

Chapter Five

Bonnie

Do not let wisdom and understanding out of your sight. Preserve sound judgment and discretion; they will be life for you, an ornament to grace your neck. Then you will go on your way in safety, and your foot will not stumble.
-Proverbs 3: 21-23

"OOOOh, you so pretty!" Bonnie said as she hugged me. I hugged her, stood back, and stared at a tall, white woman in front of me. Bonnie was beautiful. She had a bangin' body, long manicured nails, and long hair with an asymmetrical cut. I smiled at her compliment, but stared at her. Had I not been looking right at her, I would've thought I was interacting with a Black woman. "It's nice to meet you Heat, I'm Bonnie." She said smiling directly at me.

"Bonnie is my friend, Heat. You'll be seeing her around more often," my dad stated like I didn't already know what was up. "OK. It's nice to meet you Bonnie," I stated and then looked over at her son.

"It's nice to meet you too. This is my son Leo," she responded and looked over at him. Leo looked up at his mom and then over to me. He smiled, "Hey!" "Hi, nice to meet you too," I responded to Leo.

I stood there slightly confused. Daddy seemed to replace Queen and Cash in the blink of an eye. I had grown to love Queen and Cash and still didn't understand what I did wrong or how I could have helped fix things -- if I could've even helped fix it. I missed them. They had been a part of our lives for so long that I just couldn't understand why Daddy didn't seem to miss them as well.

I don't even remember exactly when Queen and Cash moved out or why. Just like Mama's funeral, decisions were made, folks fussed back and forth, and I was left to navigate the repercussions on my own. Without Queen, I had to deal with Daddy alone and he could often be cold and domineering. He was the kind of man that spoke at you but not with you. I needed the nurturing side of Queen to balance out our home. And, I unknowingly needed Cash to make me feel wanted. At that age, I didn't know if this breakup was a blessing, a curse, or both.

By 13, I learned how to keep busy as Daddy began to entertain different women in our home. It felt like he was either at work, reading how-to books and newspapers, or dealing with his women while I was pretty much raising myself. When Bonnie and her son Leo started to come around, it helped return some balance to our lives. Unlike Queen, Bonnie kept her own place and would visit us with Leo for the weekend or invite daddy and I to visit them for the weekend.

~ ~ ~

I hated being alone while daddy spent all day at work. During the weekdays I started hosting parties at the house while my Dad was at work and expecting me to be in school. I was only in middle school, but I would sit around with my friends and we would drink his beer and smoke his cigarettes. Daddy always shopped in bulk as if the store was going to stop selling whatever he liked, so I was known to keep a stash of cigarettes and beer at the crib.

Although I was barely a teenager, I remember feeling pretty grown. I was always concerned with getting attention from boys. I was a big tease though. When boys wanted me to follow up on my flirtatious behavior, I would usually disappear on them. Even though I would never follow through sexually, whenever the boys I was interested in hesitated to give me the attention I desired, I thought of them as lame and cut them off.

My homies and I had so much free time to chill out that you would have thought we were grown. We had access to smoke, drink and would simply do whatever we wanted. And, if you didn't have parents that allowed you to hang out like we were, you were wack to me.

At first, I didn't know what to expect with Bonnie and Leo. But, as I became more comfortable with having them around, they felt more and more like the family I craved. I was drawn to Bonnie. She carried herself with a confidence that reminded my dad that she didn't need him like the other women did. This intrigued my dad and ultimately intrigued me as well. She provided the loving, nurturing, and motherly vibe that I needed without seeking anything in return. I had grown used to women who would temporarily try to buy me off because they were interested in my dad, but really could care less about me.

Bonnie was different. She made an effort to spend quality time with me. She seemed to genuinely understand how lonely I was without me ever having to say a word. When daddy was working, she would take me to the movies, the park, church, and even her best friend's house. She never treated me any different from her own son and that made me feel loved. Her best friend, Yoshi, even began to call me her niece and would ask Bonnie about me when I wasn't around. It made me feel so cared for and loved. As my relationship with Bonnie strengthened, I didn't even care too much about throwing parties or talking to boys when my dad wasn't home anymore. She always had something for me to do. It was just like having a real mom, and I loved every bit of it.

~ ~ ~

"Shit, let me hurry up!" I muttered to myself as I crawled out of the bed at 10 o'clock Saturday morning to begin my Saturday chores. Leo and Bonnie were already off spending their

Saturday on the soccer field. Leo was an amazing soccer player and they would often leave early on a Saturday morning to get Leo to his games.

I walked downstairs to start my chores in the kitchen. Daddy was already at work and I knew he would be home by 3. It was my responsibility to sweep and mop the kitchen, wash and put away the dishes, clean the bathroom, and wash and fold our clothes.

I hated my Saturday chores but they earned me a weekly allowance of $25 cash and $100 that I could spend on my Rich's credit card along with permission to hang out at the mall and skating rink.

By 1:00pm I was done with my chores and immediately wanted to pick out something fly to wear. I picked out a fresh pair of Gloria Vanderbilt jeans and a cute Polo top.

Daddy pulled up from work a little after 3. He walked in the house and set his keys down on the kitchen counter. He looked around.

"OK, it looks clean in here. You did everything you were supposed to do?" He asked.

"Yes. Can I go to the mall and the skating rink?" I asked.

"Aight, let's go now cause I got to take a nap and be somewhere later." He said and picked his keys back up. Some days we would have to pick up my girls, but today we planned to just meet up at the mall. They usually preferred to ride with me because my daddy always had the newest Lincoln Continental before it even hit the sales floor. But some days, I really just didn't want him all up in my groove.

We pulled into Greenbriar Mall around 4pm. "You better not be out here with none of these lil niggas," daddy said as he handed me my $25 allowance. "And remember the spending limit on your card!"

"Whatever," I thought and started opening the door. "Aight, thanks bye," I mumbled and hopped out of the car. I looked over to the mall entrance and spotted my girls Zephoria, Tootsie, Star, and Latifah.

"SUMMMMMMMER HEEAT!" Zephoria yelled with both arms in the air.

"What's up?" I responded to Zephoria while laughing and walking towards her. Zephoria, Tootsie, Star, and Latifah were my closest friends. I felt like our lives were similar so I always felt understood by them. The five of us walked inside the mall and towards the food court.

"Y'all tryna skate? You know Talib and his boys will be up there," Latifah said.

"Hell yea! You talking about Brick and 'nem? They fine as hell. I'm going." Zephoria answered.

I laughed, "Yea that's cool. Ain't no movies out I want to see this week anyway." I walked over to the counter of my favorite pizza and wings spot. Zephoria, Tootsie, Star, and Latifah followed.

"I'm about to get a slice of pizza and an Orange ICEE," I announced. I ordered my pizza and ICEE and went to look for a table. Zephoria and Latifah stood at the counter next. Zephoria looked over at Latifah, "You got me?" "Yea, you good," Latifah replied. Zephoria looked up at the cashier, "Can I have a slice of pepperoni and a orange ICEE?" Tootsie and Star ordered last.

"Anything else?" The cashier replied.

"Yes, can I get the same thing?" Latifah asked.

"$6.38" The cashier announced.

Latifah took a balled up $10 bill out of her pocket and handed it to the cashier.

I looked over at them ordering and thought about my sisters. I pictured what it would have been like if they were closer to me in age. Would I feel as alone? Would I always have someone to have my back? For half a second, I found myself trapped in a daydream until Latifah came over to the table with both of our ICEEs. Zephoria walked behind her with her ICEE and her slice. "Y'all pizza up there," she stated as she sat down. Latifah and I got up and walked to the counter and picked up our slices. Tootsie and Star waited at the counter for their food.

The five of us sat in the food court for another two hours laughing and catching up. By the time we got to the skating rink, it was crowded just like we liked it. The skate scene had a little bit of everything going on: drama, relationships, dance groups, dry humping on the dance floor, and older guys looking for younger girls to stroke their ego. At that age, talking to older guys made us younger girls feel grown and invincible. It never occurred to anyone that it wasn't a healthy dynamic to encourage. We were just being teens.

"Ay, what's your name?" I heard a deep voice say behind me. I turned around and there he stood. The boy I was just watching who was dancing with his boys. He was a really good dancer and it intrigued me.

"What?" I responded with an attitude.

"I said, What's your name? I see you keep looking at me like you want something."

He spoke with a certain arrogance that I was attracted to and feared at the same time. I liked him instantly.

"Boy, ain't nobody thinking 'bout you. You can dance and all, but I was looking at everybody dance." I responded quickly to let him know who he was dealing with and he saw right through it.

"Aight, Aight. What's your name?" He chuckled at my teenage display of confidence.

"Call me Heat." I said staring straight at him.

"Heat? Like the weather?"

"Heat like the temperature." I replied with a smirk.

"Well, what's up Heat. I'm tryna holla at you, but you over here acting funny. My folks call me Brick."

"Brick?" I laughed. "Why they call you Brick?" I asked.

"Don't worry about all that. I wanna learn more about you."

"What you wanna know?"

"How old are you?"

"13."

"13? Your daddy let you be out here?"

"Don't worry about what my daddy let me do. How old are you? I bet you ain't even in school."

"Nah, fuck school. I'm old enough. School ain't got shit for me. Baby, I'm getting money. I learn what I need from who I need to learn it from."

His confidence was sexy to me and I was

excited that he wanted to talk to me. I craved male attention so bad by this time in my life that I had no idea that this encounter would determine the course of my future. All that time, all I knew was that he was cute, a bad boy, and interested in me.

~ ~ ~

"You talk to that boy again today?" I looked up and saw Bonnie standing at my bedroom door.

"Who Brick? Yea, I did," I responded coyly. She knew I liked him, but she was also concerned that he was so much older than me.

"OK, I'm not gonna fuss at you for talking to him, but I do want you to be careful. You see how these men are and you see how I always have to set your daddy straight. You gotta keep the upper hand with these players out here selling the same BS to every girl. I'm not with that shit."

Even though I knew Bonnie was right, I still wanted to have an older boyfriend. Boys my age were so timid, especially when it came to the stuff I was into before Bonnie came around. I respected her, but Brick and I started dating despite her disapproval. Dating a 16, almost 17, year old boy at 13? You couldn't tell me nothing.

Bonnie became the mother figure I longed for and I cherished the relationship we had. She would try to distract me from Brick by trying to find her and I something to do. I was able to talk to her about everything and even if she didn't agree with my choices, she never shamed me for them. My bond with Bonnie had gotten so tight that when daddy would be too hard on me, she'd come to the house, pack me up, and take me with her. My dad would then come over to her place with his act together. He never apologized, but he definitely changed his attitude when she spoke up. She didn't play with him and he in turn seemed to love the challenge and constantly chased after her. Their dynamic taught me a lot about relationships. I knew I wanted to have the kind of confidence and power Bonnie had. It was similar to the confidence and power I saw in my mother when I was a little girl.

At 13 I was crowned Miss Eighth Grade and my dad was the proudest of me that I had ever seen him. I was a tomboy, so I hardly wore dresses. For the eighth grade prom and homecoming, I was able to wear a pants suit as Miss Eighth Grade. But, for the coronation, I had to wear a dress.

My dad was mean but always gave me everything I wanted, especially when Bonnie was around. I never understood that about him, but I grew to accept it. One thing about him was that he was going to make sure his girls looked good. He even went to cosmetology school to learn how to do our hair.

When my dad found out that I needed a dress for the coronation, he ran out to David's Bridal and bought me a whole wedding dress. At first, I was embarrassed that he bought me a wedding dress for the coronation, but I ended up looking really cute. He topped it off by cutting my hair into an asymmetrical style similar to Bonnie's. He really made sure I looked nice for my coronation and I loved sharing that moment with him.

After the coronation, my dad asked me what I wanted as a gift for being crowned Miss Eighth Grade. I told him that I wanted a car. I was 13 without a license, but I knew how to drive. My dad agreed to it. He went to work and customized a red and a black Merkur and brought them both home for me to choose. I struggled to choose and my dad ended up just keeping both cars. He would drive the black one and I would drive the red one.

Once I started driving the red one, my dad continued to customize my car. He put in a large speaker in the back of the car and stitched my name into the headrest. As long as I was home by my curfew, I was able to ride around unsupervised.

After a while, I started to sneak out. I was all over the city with my best friend, Star. I learned how to turn the mileage back so that my dad wouldn't know how much I was driving the car. I would even make it a point to get home at least an hour or two before he did to make sure the car's engine was cool by the time he got home.

Looking back, those middle school years with my dad and Bonnie, were possibly the best years of my life after my mother passed. I felt safe, I felt loved, and even when my dad and I butt heads, he gave me everything I wanted.

~ ~ ~

"Don't call her no more."

"What? Why?" I asked my daddy.

"Do what I say," he responded.

I was confused. I hung the phone up and tossed it to the side. I was confused. A week had gone by and I hadn't heard from Bonnie. I was attempting to reach out to her when daddy stopped me. I stared at my eighth grade graduation picture on the coffee table. It was a picture of me, daddy, and Bonnie.

I looked like the Tasmanian Devil in that pic. Daddy and I had just fallen out and we both looked pissed. Bonnie, as always, was in the picture just smiling like she knew everything would be okay. I really missed her.

Daddy refused to explain to me what was going on. Once again, someone I loved was ripped from my life without explanation and it hurt deeply. I didn't understand why I had to break up with Bonnie because daddy broke up with her. I was pissed. I knew Bonnie had to miss me like I missed her, but I didn't know how to continue a relationship with her without daddy. So, I followed my daddy's instructions and I never called Bonnie again.

By the time I was 15 and Brick was 18, we were in a full blown relationship. Bonnie was a great distraction when she was around, but now that she was out of our lives I was back to looking for attention and connection wherever I could find it. Brick answered that longing.

My dad continued to work a lot leaving me with the house to myself often. Since I was 5 years old, he "trusted" me to take care of myself. It wasn't until I was an adult that I recognized that his trust consistently left me in vulnerable positions that created deep areas of hurt and shame within me. The neighbors were asked to keep an eye out so I learned how to sneak Brick in and out the house through the backyard so no one would see him coming and going.

At this point, I saw myself as a grown woman. I was breaking my daddy's rules constantly, and just doing whatever I wanted to do. And, to top it all off, I felt like I was finally experiencing the kind of relationship I envisioned with Cash when I was eleven years old.

Chapter Six

Homeless

"Children, obey your parents in the Lord, for this is right. "Honor your father and mother" (this is the first commandment with a promise), "that it may go well with you and that you may live long in the land." -Ephesians 6: 1-3

"Oh you grown? You can't do what I say do? Then you can get the hell on. You don't have to live in this house! I don't want nobody around me that don't wanna be around me."

"Fuck You!" I yelled back at my father in my head. I knew I would be dead on the scene if I yelled back at him out loud. Instead, I stood there giving him a real blank stare.

"Oh you think I won't kill you. You think you grown. You make me sick. If you can't do what I say do, you gotta go."

"OK then!" I yelled and rolled my eyes.

"Oh you talking back?"

"No." I replied lowering my voice while thinking, "I'm out of here soon as I get a chance!" I stormed upstairs.

"You can do whatever the fuck you want! If you gonna go, stay gone! You ain't got to come back here. Just make sure you keep your ass in school. If I find out your ass ain't in school, I'm gonna have your ass locked up and brought right back here to live," he shouted back.

That night I packed my bags and called my best male friend Blue. Blue's older brother was 17 with a driver's license and access to his mother's car. We planned my runaway and I hid my bags in my closet for a week. I felt like I knew how to take care of myself already and didn't need to live in my daddy's house anymore.

One day, while daddy was at work, Blue and his brother, Belly, came through to pick me up like we planned. They dropped me off at my best friend Star's house. Star's dad also worked all day like mine. Star's mom, Mrs. Lilly, allowed me to stay with them as long as I kept a job and paid her weekly. At the time, I didn't fully recognize that she was becoming a functioning addict.

By this time, I was already working at a Funpark Amusement Center and able to give Mrs. Lilly $25 a week. Star worked at Funpark with me and we learned how to make money on top of our hourly pay. I would never tell Star how much I made because she would end her night with around $200 and I would end with over $1500. I would just tell her that I made whatever she said she made and occasionally I would add $50 to whatever she said she made.

When Mrs. Lilly found out we were making extra money on the side, she immediately started asking me for more money. While I was mature enough to understand that I couldn't stay in this woman's house free of charge, there was a part of me that questioned whether or not she recognized that I was still a kid in need of a nurturing home. Mrs. Lilly gradually started asking me for more and more money each week. Twenty-five dollars per week turned into $40 turned into $60. I would even pay her an additional $50 to $60 for getting Star and I our weekend hotel rooms to host parties for our friends.

Eventually, I made enough money on the side to buy myself a car. I paid Mrs. Lily to pose as my mother and take me to get my driver's license. After getting my license and then a car, Mrs. Lilly began to act as if I was completely indebted to her. She demanded more money and rides to wherever she wanted to go. She started making threats behind Star's back attempting to extort money from me and threatening to put me out if I didn't oblige. I got tired of it and eventually… I left. I just left.

After I left, I would just stay with whoever would let me stay. No matter where I stayed, I always went to school and kept a job. The one thing I knew I had to do was graduate from high school. Not because of my father's threats, but because of my mother's wishes.

At one point I stayed with a co-worker and her mother, Ms. Gloria. Ms. Gloria was a sweet Jehovah Witness woman who did not drive. While I stayed with them I would take turns giving Ms. Gloria a ride to the bus stop or train station before school. I always felt safe in their home because they were so kind to me when they did not have to be.

I was careful not to bring too much attention to Ms. Gloria's home. I still hung out with Star on a regular basis, but I would go pick her up and we would go hang out around town. Mrs. Lilly would rent us a hotel room on the weekends when we wanted to party late with our friends. Of course we had a price to pay her to book the rental. If we didn't oblige to her request, we got CUSSED out, and would still end up paying her to rent the rooms for us. Ultimately, we felt like it was well worth it.

I left Ms. Gloria's the day after my boyfriend at the time threatened to kill me. I felt that my volatile relationship with him was putting them in danger. So, again, I just left.

I found myself staying wherever I could lay my head for a moment. There were even times where I would stay in my car and bathe at school. I befriended the custodian at my high school and he would allow me in the building to shower and get dressed in the locker room before school. My car had a hatchback so I would hide my stuff in there before school so no one could tell that I was living out of the car.

After a good while, I got tired of living from pillar to post. I called my older sister Autumn and asked if I could stay with her for awhile. By this time Autumn was married and living in another county. She knew I had left home, but she didn't know the extent of what I was going through. I felt so abandoned by everyone that it was hard for me to ask anyone for anything. My sisters were so much older than me and well into their adult lives. I felt like they completely forgot about me. But, now that I was struggling and exhausted, I had no choice but to reach out.

When Autumn told me I could stay with her, I transferred to the high school in her neighborhood and started school there. I didn't anticipate hating the high school in her neighborhood as much as I did. I missed my friends that I had been with since elementary and middle school. I only ended up making only one real friend who I later moved in with.

~ ~ ~

"You new?" Brooklyn said looking at me.

"Yes." I said glaring back at her.

"What's your name?" She asked.

"Heat."

"Heat? I know that ain't your real name."

"It is. My name is Summer Heat," I replied slightly irritated.

I wasn't feeling this girl already. There I was, sitting in the back of my new math class minding my business and here she was, all in my face asking questions. I really wanted to tell her to mind her business, but I didn't know anyone for real yet so I kept it cool and just responded with one or two words.

"Oh OK then Summer Heat. Well, I'm

Brooklyn. You like Math?" She asked.

"Yea, it's alright," I responded.

"Cool, cause I need somebody to do my homework for this class," she smirked.

I looked at her. She had the wrong one.

"Why? Cause you run track or something?" I said looking at the team logo on her jacket.

She snickered, "Yea, I don't have time for homework and I hate math. You can be the one to do my homework for this class."

I looked over at Brooklyn like she was crazy and looked away. I couldn't believe she really had the nerve to ask me to do her work because I was new.

It was at that moment I realized that after everything I'd been through at this point, there was no way I was about to take shit from a self-absorbed track star. My life wasn't the typical "teen" life and I didn't have time for the Nickelodeon bullshit that I felt she was on.

After a couple weeks of trying to get me to do her work, Brooklyn got loud in front of the class and stated that I would be doing all her work from here on out. It was clear she thought she was funny and that her popularity made her invincible. She didn't realize that she had the wrong one.

By this time, I started hanging out with

Shai. Shai was my one friend at my new school and she did not like Brooklyn either. That evening after Brooklyn tried to showboat in front of the class, we devised a plan to jump Brooklyn in the student parking lot the next day.

The next day, Shai and I sat in my car watching the other students pull up to school. Sitting in the student parking lot you could see what kids were secretly well off but tried to act hard, those who were taking care of themselves, and those who were just trying to be on the scene.

We watched Brooklyn pull up to the school in an old Dodge Shadow. Our plan was in motion. I looked around to make sure no teachers or administrators were around while Shai tried to see inside the car to make sure she was alone. When it was clear, we simultaneously stepped out of the car. We walked towards Brooklyn's car casually as if we were walking towards the side entrance of the school building. As we approached the car, Brooklyn opened her car door and stepped out. As soon as her car door shut, Shai and I rushed Brooklyn and started whooping her ass.

Shai and I continued to tag-team Brooklyn as a crowd gathered around us with kids yelling and laughing. Shai then made sure no one else jumped in and let me finish her off. I had no idea how much time had passed by the time an administrator and the school security officer ran outside to break up the fight.

~ ~ ~

I sat in the front office pissed. Everyone immediately jumped to Brooklyn's defense. Here it was, this chick who could not even read and bullied other kids to do her homework was coddled because she offered something to the school. While here I was facing expulsion at a time I needed adult support the most. I felt worthless.

The whole ordeal took a turn for the worse when I was told that my father needed to come to the school because I was going to be expelled. I was living with Shai and her mom at this time and hadn't needed any parental representation until now.

My father was pissed. After they explained the conditions of my expulsion, my dad signed the paperwork and we left. I knew he was still upset about me leaving, but would barely look at me much less speak. As we walked out of the school building, I walked to my car and he walked to his.

Chapter Seven

Seventeen

Train up a child in the way he should go: and when he is old, he will not depart from it.
-Proverbs 23:6

I ENDED UP HAVING TO GO TO ATLANTA Alternative School after I was expelled. AAS was the school you went to if you were expelled, pregnant, or married. You could enroll and withdraw yourself so there were also adults there who just wanted to go back to school and get their traditional diploma. The classes were like an hour and 50 minutes long. You could only miss 3 days or 6 half days each quarter. If you missed more than 3 days, they didn't call your parents, you would just be automatically un-enrolled.

I did well at AAS. One of my best friends from my previous high school, Zephoria, was there because she had a baby. It felt good to be around a familiar face that I could trust outside of Shai. Zephoria and I became each other's motivation to finish high school.

I only had three quarters left to complete for my diploma. Mama's dying wish was that I got my high school diploma and I was determined to do that. I ended up finishing high school six months earlier than the average student my age. I knew she would be proud.

I went back and graduated with my friends at Clairmont. Since I was six months ahead, I was able to sit out the final semester and work extra hours until graduation day.

My dad came to my graduation. I didn't expect him but I was happy he came. I didn't let him know that though. When I caught up with him after the ceremony, we exchanged a dry hello, a cold embrace, and went our separate ways. There never seemed to be any words that could fill the distance between us. Of course by this time I had been on my own for two years.

Shortly after graduation, I was looking to move out of Shai's mother's house. Shai and

I fell out and she had one time to remind me of what she had done for me and I was gone. I went to live with my oldest sister Reign after leaving Shai's. I didn't really know where I belonged so I spent a lot of time just being out and about. The one thing I had was my car, and I loved the autonomy it allowed me to have. So, I would just ride around.

One day while riding around, I spotted Brick posted up in front of a store laughing with two other dudes. I slowed down.

"Brick! Brick!" I yelled and popped the horn twice. "Brick!" I continued to yell. Brick turned his head slowly in my direction. Startled, I waved wildly at him.

"Oh shit Heat??"

"Yes Nigga! How you doing?"

"I can't call it. I heard you were up on the other side of town now. What you doing over here?"

"I'm back, I'm staying with Reign now so I'll be around."

"Word? OK, well let's connect. What's your number?"

I gave Brick my number and we parted ways. As I drove off I reminisced about the time I spent with Brick before leaving my Daddy's house and how much I loved him then. It was at that moment I figured he had to be my soulmate so I couldn't wait to see him again.

My relationship with Brick picked back up like it never ended. The only problem was that he now had two children--a one year old and a 3 year old. Here it was, I was 17 going on 18, barely out of high school, and dating a grown 21-year-old man with kids. At the time, I just felt like an adult anyway. I was already living by my own rules. I felt like I didn't even know how to be a teenager anymore... if I had ever had the chance to be one in the first place.

I started staying with Brick at his grandfather's house. Since I was staying with them, we started moving like we were a married couple. So, on the day after my 17th birthday, we got married.

~ ~ ~

"Alright, I'll call you back later," I heard Brick whisper on the phone as I walked into a kitchen.

"Was that your baby mama?" I asked him pretending not to notice the smile that was on his face.

"Yea, that was Barbeesha. She's gonna bring the baby over here Friday night." He responded.

Something told me that there was more

to it than that by the way he was whispering and smiling when I entered the room, but I told myself that I was overreacting. After all, we had known each other long before both his baby mamas came into the picture. In my young, naive mind I was the wife so I was winning.

That Friday night Barbeesha brought the baby over as expected. I knew she didn't like me and I didn't feel like dealing with her attitude so I sat and watched them from the kitchen.

"Heat in there?" I heard her ask Brick.

"Yea she home." He responded.

Barbeesha muttered a response and passed Brick his son. "Alright, I'll bring him home Sunday afternoon," Brick said.

The door closed and I got up and walked over to Brick and his son, RaQuan.

"Hey RaRa," I said as Brick sat RaQuan on the couch.

"Heeeet!" he said and reached his arms towards me. As I played with Brick's son, he sat down on the armchair next to us.

"Heat, I'm gonna need to run out in about 10 minutes. Can you watch RaQuan for a little bit?"

"What's a little bit?" I asked, recognizing that this was the third time in a row I was left at home with his baby and his grandfather.

"Only about an hour, damn." He answered with an attitude. Trying to avoid an argument, I just stared at him. Brick stood up and walked upstairs. I heard the shower run as he started getting ready for wherever he was planning to go.

About 20 minutes later, Brick walked into the kitchen where I was putting together a snack for his son. He grabbed my car keys from the kitchen table and walked towards the door.

"Aight RaRa, I'll be right back!" Brick said to his son and left. It wasn't long before I realized what was happening. I would soon find out Brick and Barbeesha were still together and they were having me watch the baby while they hooked up. I was livid. I thought back to the day I was in the car when my mom found out my dad was cheating. Was this normal in marriages? I felt like the patterns and lifestyle we were creating was not what I expected marriage to look like. Life was moving so much faster than my 17-year-old mind was prepared for.

Chapter Eight

Brick

When the righteous cry for help, the Lord hears,
and rescues them from all their troubles.
-Psalms 34:17

"Where did you say you were sending this package?"

"Germany." I replied.

I stood at the shipping counter in the Post Office shaking with anger as I watched the postal worker stamp "AIR MAIL" on my package. I couldn't believe that I caught Brick cheating again. Brick's other baby mama and his daughter, Charlene, went out to Germany to visit Charlene's mother and husband.

Charlene, knowing that Brick was at least in a relationship, had the nerve to send him a letter from Germany talking about "I love you, I miss you, I thought you were going to leave her." I was livid. After all this time, he hadn't even let his exes know that we were actually married. I was so mad that I found every picture and every item of clothing that she had ever given him and cut it up. After I cut up the photos, shirts, pants, etc. I put it all in a box and mailed it to the return address in Germany.

~ ~ ~

"Heat!!! Why the hell would you send them that shit?" Brick yelled as I walked in the house a couple weeks later. I smirked to myself. The package must have arrived.

Charlene and her mother were now just as angry as I was. Charlene's mother called Brick and cussed him out for marrying me. She boldly asked him "how you go and marry that bitch and let her send us that shit." It was one thing for Brick to be cheating, but to have these women that didn't really know me talking about me in all kinds of ways pissed me off even more. Instead of recognizing that he was caught up in a lie, Brick got mad at me for sending the box.

"You should've told her you were married. She sending you shit about leaving me, so I sent some shit too." I responded.

I stared at him waiting for a response. He stared at me with a blank look.

I continued. "Shit, matter of fact, don't ask me why I sent that package over there, ask her why she sent that letter over here. This my address too!"

Brick didn't have an answer for me. He knew he was wrong. "Whatever. You trippin," he mumbled and walked off.

~ ~ ~

"Is Brick here?" A woman's voice called from the front door.

"Who you here to see?" I asked walking back towards the front door. I had just walked in the door and had barely had a chance to put my things down and go close the door.

"Brick." She replied.

"Who are you?"

"His Girl!" She replied getting agitated.

"His Girl?? Honey, I'm his wife!!! Didn't he tell you he was married!"

She paused and stared at me. Clearly embarrassed.

"No! I can't believe this nigga!" She said.

In that moment I knew Brick was the problem, not the woman at my door who didn't know I existed until now. I was livid once again. There was a certain familiarity I felt with the painful disappointment in her eyes. She liked him and this hurt her.

I thought about Bonnie. She never liked Brick. She would always tell me that I needed to keep the upper hand because men would sell the same BS to as many women as they could. So, in that moment, I came up with a plan.

"Yep. That nigga's a liar, girl. You ain't the first and probably won't be the last. I'll tell you what. He'll be off work at 5:30. Can you please come back here at 5:45 on the dot?"

"Yea! I gotchu. I'll be back." She said regaining her composure and walked towards her car.

At 5:45PM, Brick's girlfriend came back like we agreed.

Bam. Bam. Bam.

"BRICK!!" She yelled while pounding on the door.

I hopped up ready for the show. "Come on Brick! Somebody out here looking for you!" I said walking towards the door.

"Man, I ain't going out there! I don't know who the fuck that is." Brick shouted back at me. I knew he was lying and he knew he was caught.

"BRICK!! IF YOU DON'T COME OUT HERE I'M GOING TO STAB YOUR ASS!" She yelled.

Brick hopped up and came to the door.

"Ain't this your girlfriend Brick?" I asked.

"Girlfriend? Nah! Girl I don't know you!" He yelled peering through the screen door.

Her mouth dropped. For a second, she looked like she was about to cry.

"Fuck You Brick! You don't know me now?" She yelled.

"Ma'am, you see he silly. He play games all day. Go on and free yourself!" I responded to her.

"You damn right. Fuck that nigga!" She turned and started walking towards her car. I turned and looked at Brick. He did not say a word. He just turned around and walked back in the house. He knew he was caught, but he held onto that lie like she and I were the crazy ones.

At this point in our marriage, I realized that it would always be something with Brick and I often wondered if this is what my mother,

Queen, and Bonnie experienced with my Dad. I was home everyday while he was at work, so to the outside world it seemed that I was living the perfect housewife life, but inside I was miserable.

Thinking back to my father's dealings with women, I started to believe that Brick's infidelity was a normal part of being married. I told myself that this was the consequence of dating the popular bad boy that everyone loved and I would just have to learn to accept it if I wanted him to be with me.

Chapter Nine

Freda

The Lord rescues the godly; he is their fortress in times of trouble. The Lord helps them, rescuing them from the wicked. He saves them, and they find shelter in him.
-Psalm 37: 39-40

Brick and I lived in his grandfather's house a few minutes away from his mother's apartment. The more acquainted I got with Brick and his family, the more things started to seem off. For example, Brick was not allowed at his mom's house without someone being at home. I thought it was mainly because he was in and out of juvenile, but I never really questioned it.

Since I was at home everyday, Brick's

mother asked me to keep an eye on his younger, 12-year-old sister, Freda, after school. She only needed me to go down to her apartment and stay with her until her parents came home.

Freda was not the typical rebellious preteen. She was a lot more. She was a beautiful girl who craved the attention of young men. She was in middle school, but looked like she was already in high school. Older boys would knock on the door after school and she would leave with them and come back drunk.

Often, when I was babysitting Freda, I would end up having to sober her up before her parents got home. At first, I didn't understand why she behaved the way she did. I kept thinking that she was too pretty to keep putting herself out there like that. It took me a minute to remember that I was just like Freda at that age… and why. Someone had prematurely awakened this girl's sexual nature without care in the same way that mine had been awakened. Now, she was out here vying for the attention of older boys like it was normal.

Freda's promiscuity and rebellion intensified the more time she spent around her older cousin Keshia. Keshia was the one to introduce Freda to having relations with older men. The family knew that Keshia was a bad influence, but it didn't seem to occur to anyone that there may have been more going on with Freda, and Keshia, than they realized. In hindsight, all the signs of child molestation were there, but I suppose it was easier for people to label both girls as fast without trying to figure out why. Folks just did not like to talk about the inappropriate interactions of an uncle, cousin, brother, or father. And, they still don't.

Keshia was not the only bad influence in Freda's life. Whenever I would supervise Freda's sleepovers, she and her neighborhood friend Kelly would get into all kinds of trouble. Not only would they sneak out of the window and run the streets, but one day they poured out half of Freda's father's Hennessy and filled it back up with lighter fluid. Freda ended up confessing after a few days that she did it because she wanted to kill her father.

Years later Freda would end up in the hospital after getting sick from an untreated gonorrhea infection. After a second trip to the hospital for the second untreated infection, she was told that she would never be able to have children.

I thought about Freda often. At times I saw myself in her and wanted to protect her from all the things I went through. Freda's behavior should have been another red flag about Brick, the way he was raised, and why they both acted out the way they did. I wondered who could have been messing with her at an early age. Could it have been Brick? Why wasn't he allowed to watch her or be at the house alone? Could it have been the father that she wanted to kill? Why did she even want to kill him? Another family member? Could it have been a family friend?

Based on my own experience, I was sure that it was something outside of her control that she would never tell a soul. Now, here she was, facing infertility after a lifetime of battling demons that she never asked for.

Chapter Ten

Shoshanna

I am the rose of Shoshanna, and the lily of the valleys. As the lily among thorns, so is my love among the daughters.
-Song of Solomon 2:2

"Summer? Uh, Summer Heat?"

"Yes?" I said hesitantly into the phone. The deep, authoritative voice on the other end told me immediately that this call was going to have something to do with Brick. I put my hand on my womb and breathed deeply.

"Hey. This is Officer Morgan calling from the homicide unit. Your husband has just been arrested and we need you to come pick up his car. He told us you were pregnant and needed the car. You have 30 minutes to come get it or else it will be impounded."

My jaw dropped. If it wasn't one thing with Brick, it was another. He couldn't seem to stay away from the ladies or out of trouble. Here I was eight months pregnant and he was getting ready to do time.

Later that night I found out Brick was caught up in an altercation with some guys at his mother's apartment complex. He shot one dude 13 times. The guy survived but ended up in critical condition. Once I heard the whole story, I knew I would be giving birth to our daughter alone. I rubbed my womb again. Frustrated. I couldn't seem to catch a break.

"I'll be there in 30 minutes," I told Officer Morgan dryly and hung up. I called my sister Reign to take me to the station to get the car. I knew I would need it to get back and forth to doctor's appointments without Brick, so getting the car was not an option. Reign picked me up and took me to the station. When we got there they wouldn't let me see Brick, but they did give me the car. They handed me the keys, asked me to sign a few papers, and then told me where the car was parked. I hopped in the car and pulled off. Frustrated.

I didn't want to stay in Brick's grandfather's house while Brick was in jail, so I left the house and moved in with Reign. I was eight months pregnant so Reign became my number one support while he was gone. In a matter of a few days, my lifestyle changed. I went from being a housewife with no real bills to working two jobs: Dial's Pizza by day and packing baseball cards in a warehouse at night.

I visited Brick in jail up until he was sentenced. He was found guilty of aggravated assault and was sentenced to five years.

I gave birth to our daughter a few weeks into his sentence. Reign was by my side as always. My dad, who didn't care for Brick at all, stopped by the hospital briefly with a beautiful bouquet of lilies.

"I think I want to name her Shoshanna." I told Reign.

"Shoshanna? I just knew you were gonna name her Winter or something. Why Shoshanna?" Reign asked.

"I read it in the Bible. It means lily. Like lily of the valley," I paused and looked over at the lilies daddy had dropped off. "Daddy still loves me even though he don't like everything I do… look at those lilies he brought me." I didn't know how to explain it. It just felt right.

Reign smiled. "Girl, that's cause you spoiled." We laughed. I never felt as spoiled as my sisters saw me.

"You know what I'm saying though Reign!" I responded.

"Yes Summer Heat. I do. Shoshanna it is."

~ ~ ~

One month after Shoshanna, who we nicknamed Shosh, was born, I dressed her up and took her to meet her father for the first time. We were only able to talk through the glass so he wasn't able to hold her or touch her. It hurt that we couldn't be the family I wanted us to be or that they couldn't form a true father-daughter bond. I wanted him to know and love Shosh like he did his other children.

While Brick was in jail, I decided to move out of Reign's house. I loved my sister dearly, but after Shosh was born, I didn't want to be a burden. I went and got an apartment with my childhood friend Coko.

Coko was a year under me in school. We were cool, but we had different groups of friends. At this time, Coko was attending Clark Atlanta University and working at Mr. Chick's. I, on the other hand, was working at the airport and sending Shosh to daycare.

Coko and I made a pact not to move

anyone else into the apartment. She had her room and Shosh and I had a room. Folks were allowed to come and go, but with Shosh being my priority, moving in friends and boyfriends was out of the question.

Coko and I would have folks at the house all the time. My friends like to come kick it with me. We'd smoke, I'd cook for everybody, and we'd just laugh and chill. Shosh would either be upstairs playing with her toys or at the daycare.

Coko was dating a guy named Rakim at the time. Rakim's dad was a big time drug dealer, so he supplied the weed for our frequent get-togethers. Every time people would come over the first thing they would ask about was the weed. I always smoked for free since I was cooking and providing the space to chill, but I would reach out to Rakim for him to bring us some weed.

"How often these niggas be over here?" Rakim asked. I laughed. "Every time I call you, they here or about to come through."

"Man.. Y'all buy so much from me, you could be making this money yourself."

"Whatchu mean?" I asked, looking confused.

"I'll tell you what, the next time they get ready to come over here, call me ahead of time.

Let me know how much y'all trying to spend and I'll show you something. I'm gonna put you on to something."

I knew a little about the game, but I didn't really know all of what he was talking about. I stood there dumbfounded and naive, but I wasn't above making some extra money to see about me and Shosh.

"OK cool," I said and left it at that until the next time they were getting ready to come over.

~ ~ ~

"Heat, we wanna come through there tomorrow. You gonna get some smoke for us?"

"Yea, how much y'all trying to spend."

"Like 200."

"OK, I got you."

I called Rakim immediately. He was at the house in 10 minutes.

"Ra, they got about 200 they want to spend."

"OK. I'll tell you what. I'll sell you this, and give you this." Rakim handed me $500 worth of weed and several bags.

"I'ma show you how to break this down," he said as he pointed at the weed. "You can give them this for $200 and sell the rest to whoever is asking for it. You can be discreet and let them think they still getting it from me, but this is yours to hold and make money off of."

"OK," I said in a low voice as I processed what he was setting me up with. It seemed so simple. It didn't really register that I was in the midst of signing up to be a drug dealer.

That night, I sold all of the weed Rakim sold me. I broke it down the way Rakim showed me and ended up making $1,000 on the $500 I bought it for. I actually thought that I would just be getting back a little more than the same $500 I spent. I got nervous because I wasn't expecting to make that much money.

"Ra, I got too much money. I sold it like you showed me, but I was only expecting around the same $500 back."

Rakim laughed at how green I was.

"That's how it's supposed to work shorty. You got rid of that shit fast."

"Yea I had a few more folks coming through that wanted to buy. I was sold out in a few hours," I said feeling proud of myself.

"Damn. We could make a killin' with this shit," he paused. "One thing though, we can't tell Coko about this. You know how she is."

"Yea, I know! I won't say nothing," I responded. I held out the $1,000.

"You trying to spending this whole $1,000?" He asked.

"Nah. Just $500 again," I responded and counted out $500. I was still kind of naive so I wasn't sure if he was about to let me keep the money or what. When I realized the money was mine, I was ready to do it again.

I bought my next $500 worth of weed from Ra and was sold out that same night. In one week I made almost $5,000 flipping $500 to $1,000 multiple times a day. Ra was running to bring me new product every day, sometimes multiple times a day.

"Man, I can't keep running over here, you gonna need to buy more at one time the way you selling out."

"OK, give me $1,000 worth."

"Nah, you hot right now. You need more than that. Give me $4,000."

"Damn that's a lot of money Ra. I don't know."

"Trust me, Heat."

So, I did. I counted out $4,000 cash and handed it to Rakim for $4,000 worth of weed. That stash lasted me a good while. I was able to flip it, catch up on my bills, buy groceries, and just maintain on my own. I made enough money that I stopped having to call Reign to help me out every month. I felt like I was finally making it on my own again.

At this point, Coko still had no idea what was going on. She would see me and Rakim talking and just ask what we were talking about. We would play it off as just talking shit, but her inquiries were enough to make us change the way we moved around her. Instead of bringing weed to the house, I would go and meet Rakim at his dad's house when I needed to re-up and we would just handle our business there.

My side hustle with Rakim ran smoothly until the day Coko and I fell out. Our lease was almost up and I noticed that Rakim was low-key staying with us. Now, Rakim and I were cool, but Coko and I had an agreement that no one would move in.

"Coko, we gotta talk," I said to Coko one day after Rakim left the house.

"About what?" She answered.

"You know me and Rakim cool, but we said we wasn't gonna move nobody in. If he's gonna be staying here with you, then we gotta look at splitting the rent 3 ways."

Coko instantly flared up. She was one to get worked up about the smallest things, so I knew we were about to argue about this.

"Three ways?? Well if that's the case then we need to split it four ways because your daughter live here too!" She responded getting loud and defensive.

"Bitch, what? My daughter is my child. She can't work. Rakim is a whole grown man!" Coko pissed me off when she brought my daughter into the conversation as if she were a grown woman with a job.

The argument continued and before you knew it, Coko called Rakim to hype him up about me not wanting him there. She missed the whole point about her not honoring our agreement and started getting messy. Before you knew it, Coko and I were throwing blows in the middle of our living room.

At the time my homegirl Star lived around the corner from us with her parents. She kept a spare key to the apartment just in case I was ever locked out. While Coko was on the phone feeding Rakim all kinds of lies, I called Star to vent. Star had a way of knowing when shit was about to go down. A few minutes into the fight, Star opened the front door and pulled me off of Coko.

"Fuck you bitch!" Coko yelled and ran into her room. I knew she was happy as hell that Star walked in and got me off of her.

I wasn't about to have Shosh stay in that apartment with us after the knock out drag out with Coko's ass, so I packed our stuff that night and moved back in with my sister. I left Coko and Rakim to figure out the remaining months of the lease on their own.

~ ~ ~

After Shosh turned 3, Brick was released from jail. Instead of going back to his grandfather's house, he came to live with Shosh and I at Reign's house. I continued to work at the airport and he got a job doing construction building an elementary school. We stayed with my sister until we could get our own apartment.

It wasn't long before Brick was back to his old ways. I started to find all kinds of letters that were written to him by other women while he was locked up. One day, he took the car and left me and Shosh at home. Something didn't feel right so after he got home, I checked the car to see where he had been. Sure enough, I found random lipstick and other forgotten items that had belonged to other women. I couldn't believe that after everything that had happened between us, he was back to his old games.

After Brick did time, I started to notice that he was getting even more bold with his infidelity. He was picking up females in my car, taking late night calls, etc. To make matters worse, he didn't even really care to hide it from me anymore. Every day he seemed to grow more apathetic and more aggressive about the smallest things. And, now that we had a toddler in the mix, it was becoming too much.

The cheating started to wear tight on me. Different women were popping up constantly and offering me unsolicited information about Brick and their relations with him. We would argue nonstop. Things took a turn for the worse the day he decided to put a 12 gauge shotgun in my mouth and threaten my life.

"I'll kill you, bitch!" He shouted as I felt the cold metal on my lips.

I froze. I never expected it to get this bad. My mind started racing. I didn't know what to do. I started praying out loud. I laid out and put on a show that scared him enough to back up.

"MAMA! Don't let him kill me!" I hollered.

I couldn't breathe. I felt like I was hallucinating. As soon as he thought I was seeing visions of my deceased mother, he calmed down.

"I'm sorry Heat, I'm so sorry. I'm sorry." He cried, kneeling on the floor next to me and pulling me into his arms.

"I'll never do it again. I love you. Please don't leave me. I'm so sorry." He sobbed onto my shoulder.

That was the initial breaking point for me. I had Shosh to think about now and I didn't want her to grow up thinking this is what marriage was supposed to be like. I found myself entangled in so much confusion because ultimately, I loved him. He was somewhat like a High School Sweetheart. I had been with this man since I was 13 years old. He was a bad boy for sure, but I never thought he'd hurt me. We had had many fist fights and I never felt fearful until the day he put that gun in my mouth. I never really felt like I was in danger either because I never just let him hit me. I always fought him back. I was desperately stuck between loving this man and fearing that one day he would take my life.

Brick was on edge for the rest of the day. If I wanted to go to the store, he wanted to come. If I wanted to use the restroom, I had to leave the door open. He was so afraid that I would leave him or call the police because of what he had done. This was not the life I wanted, but I ended up just trying to forget it and move on. I told myself to let it go and I stayed.

The final straw came the day Shosh, Brick, and I were visiting his mother and sister at his mother's house. Brick had a way of getting upset with me for no reason and then pleading for me not to leave him immediately after. Without any warning or obvious trigger, Brick grabbed me by the hair and dragged me out of the house, onto the porch, down four steps to the middle of the yard, and proceeded to beat me.

"*MOMMA!! MOMMA!!* "I heard Shosh crying from the porch as Brick proceeded to throw blow after blow.

Brick's mother and sister held Shosh back from running towards me and her father, but they never once intervened or told Brick to stop. They watched him beat me while they held my daughter who was also watching. I laid there bleeding from my mouth and it was like they didn't even care. All I could think was, what have I gotten myself into? How could a mother watch her son beat his wife right on her front lawn? How could Freda watch her brother beat the sister-in-law that covered for her all the times she came home drunk or found herself in trouble? I was angry, hurt, confused, and alone. I can't go through this, I told myself. I can't let my daughter see this. I knew I had to leave him.

After the fight, I was still expected to go home with Brick like a happy family. His mother and sister showed me where they stood as women and I never forgot that. I had to put an immediate exit plan in place.

I went home terrified that he would kill me if I stayed and terrified that he would kill me if he knew I was leaving. I pretended to forgive him and brush off the incident. I felt disgusted allowing him to lay next to me and hold me all night. I laid there with my eyes wide open all night while he slept like a baby. I felt like a prisoner.

That morning, I set my plan in motion. I took Brick to work, told him I loved him, and dropped Shoshanna off at daycare. I called my brother-in-law and told him what happened. Fortunately, Brick and I had just found a new apartment and had not completely moved in and settled down. This made it easy to pick up and move out.

My brother-in-law met me at the apartment and had my things moved out in two hours. Brick and I had just gotten a waterbed, but I didn't even care about that bed anymore. I took the wood panels from around the bed, and then stabbed the waterbed and flooded the apartment.

After we got everything situated, I picked Shoshanna up from daycare and went to my friend Cookie's house. I knew my sister's house would be the first place Brick would look for us, and I didn't want to put my sister and brother-in-law in the middle of our mess.

911. 911.

By 4:00 PM, my pager was blowing up. I knew it was Brick. My heart was beating so fast as he paged me back to back. I couldn't breathe. My fear of him was real. I was afraid like he was right there trying to kick the door in, even though I knew he was miles away.

I woke up the next morning and dropped Shoshanna off at daycare. I wanted to make sure that her routine remained as normal as possible. I felt the responsibility of protecting her from the mess I had found myself in with her father. I went to work after dropping Shosh off and then picked her back up after my shift. As soon as I was leaving the daycare, Brick popped up. I lost it.

"*HELP ME!!! HELP ME!!!!*" I yelled.

Three men at the daycare ran out and warned Brick to get off of their property immediately. They didn't ask questions. They saw that Shoshanna and I were in danger and stepped in to protect us. Two of the men walked Brick to the end of the street, while one stayed back with me and asked if I was okay. When the other men returned, I told them all what happened and why I was so frightened. They got me and Shoshanna in the car and watched us pull off. They stood there watching me to make sure that Brick didn't pull off until I was out of sight.

Being that afraid of anyone was not how I wanted to live my life. I was terrified. I was shaking the entire way home. I filed charges, but later dropped them once we were in court. I hated that I loved him.

Chapter Eleven

Tigga

The husband should fulfill his marital duty to his wife, and likewise the wife to her husband.
-I Corinthians 7:3

"Let's get a room. Ain't Shosh at your sister's house?"

"Boy. No." I was serious, but I laughed a bit to keep things light. "I really just need you to buy your daughter some shoes."

Phht. Brick sighed. "Aight, I'll see what I can do."

As Brick drove me home, I sat in silence staring out the window. I could tell he was disappointed and I stayed quiet to make sure that his disappointment didn't turn to rage. Brick never took rejection well and I wasn't in the mood to fight. The hardest part for me was being in love with someone who I knew was no good for me or my daughter. I struggled with my heart and my mind constantly. For whatever reason, I still craved his love and attention and I stared out of that car window thinking how much I hated loving him.

Brick had insisted that no matter what, he would take care of Shoshanna. After all my nights and weekends babysitting his other children, I wanted to believe he would. Brick, however, never did anything for Shosh without some type of negotiation. I would have to agree to go out with him just to get Shosh her basic necessities. He would consistently offer to get a room or ask to spend the night anytime I agreed to go out. He often wanted to parade around his friends and family like we were still together and would beg me to attend gatherings with him. To make sure that Shosh was taken care of, I would accept his invites but I would always find a way to get him to stop and get her some clothes or a pair of shoes. That was the only time he'd agree to taking care of his daughter as he promised.

It took me a minute to leave Brick alone but eventually, I did. I told him that I was done and as long as he left me alone, I would leave him alone. After doing time, I knew Brick didn't want any unnecessary attention brought onto him from the law, so it was easier to stay away from him than I thought. But, even though I was through with Brick, I wasn't quite ready to go through with the process of getting a divorce.

Once I left Brick alone, my father started communicating with me again. My father didn't like Brick and didn't want me to have anything to do with him, so marrying Brick and having a child with him drove an even bigger wedge between my father and I. My sisters were also glad that I was done with him and were ready for me to move on with my life. So, I did.

~ ~ ~

"Heat, it's this dude I want you to meet. He got money and I know he will take good care of you and Shosh," Stormi said.

"Girl, whatever, I'm not thinking about trying to find another dude right now," I responded.

Stormi was still struggling with her addiction and I would often go and visit her. I would take her clothes, money, and anything else I thought she needed. One day while I was visiting, Stormi insisted that I meet her supplier's boss, Tigga.

"Drive us up the street real quick. Let me see if he up there. I want y'all to meet." Reluctantly, I drove up the street with Shosh in the backseat. I figured I'd entertain her a bit and then keep it moving.

"Slow down, there he go," Stormi said. I pulled up next to a group of dudes standing next to a clean, white Lexus.

"TIGGAAA!! TIGGA! Tigga, what's up this my baby sister Heat and her daughter Shosh! They single!" Stormi shouted out of the passenger side window. I looked over at her and whispered, "Heifer, are you crazy?" She turned and laughed.

Tigga walked over to the car. "What's up Heat and Shosh?" Tigga said, looking at me and then in the backseat at Shosh. At that moment, Tigga's phone rang.

"Yeah!" He answered, put his finger up, and turned away from the car. I knew that meant he was handling business and it was attractive to me. I sat up peeking all into his car while Stormi chatted with the other dudes that were standing around. I knew he was much older than me, but when I looked at his clothes and the way he carried himself, he didn't seem much older at all. I found myself slightly interested in him.

Tigga got off the phone and walked back over to the car. "Hey y'all I gotta run. Stormi, it was good seeing you. Heat here go my number, hit me up later." Tigga walked around his Lexus and hopped in.

That evening, I was still hanging with Stormi when she dialed his number and handed me the phone. "Here, talk to him!" Stormi said. I laughed. She really wanted me to talk to this man!

"Yeah! Hello?" Tigga answered.

"Hey!" I said not really knowing what to say. "It's Heat. Stormi's sister. I met you earlier."

"Yeah I remember. The beautiful woman with her daughter that pulled up with Stormi."

I blushed and laughed a little. It felt good to be complimented like that. We chatted for a bit before he said, "You wanna go out to eat tomorrow?"

"Yea, that's cool," I said shyly.

"OK, I'll come pick y'all up tomorrow."

I got off the phone elated. He actually said "y'all" as in Me & Shoshanna. I was surprised that he didn't even question my daughter coming along. I was definitely interested now.

Tigga picked us up the following day and took Shosh and I out to eat. He treated us so well, I wanted to be with him instantly. After that, we were inseparable.

Tigga was the man around the streets. Whatever he wanted, he could have. In just six months, he changed our whole lives. When we got together, Shosh and I were still staying with Reign but I was ready to move out. I found an apartment for Shosh and I that was in the hood. I knew it wasn't the best neighborhood, but it was all I could afford on my manager's salary at McDonald's. When we moved, Tigga completely furnished my apartment. The inside looked like a high-rise condo in Buckhead and not the hood that I was actually in. He even bought me a washer and dryer combo that we had to hook up to the sink since the apartment didn't have washer/dryer hookups.

Tigga was doing so much for me that I felt like I needed to tell him about Brick. I let Tigga know that I still hadn't gotten a divorce and gave him the rundown of my relationship with Brick.

"You know what, fuck him. You don't need to worry about him. Don't call him no more for shit. I'm gonna take care of you and Shosh. We gonna be a family," Tigga responded. Tigga had a way about him that you knew he meant what he said, when he said it. After dealing with Brick, that comforted me. He did not have a problem with me still being married as long as I understood that he too was unhappily married with children. His boys were older, but he was still an active part of their lives.

Tigga kept his promise and we became a family. He took care of Shoshanna like she was his own child. Whatever she needed, he delivered. He picked her up from school and even attended PTA meetings when I couldn't. He became the father I knew she needed despite him having a family of his own. For the first time, I experienced a relationship without volatility and abuse and as long as he was there for us, I wasn't even thinking about Brick or that marriage.

CHAPTER TWELVE

The Mortuary

"Watch out for false prophets. They come to you in sheep's clothing, but inwardly they are ferocious wolves."
-Matthew 7:15

THE WAY TIGGA TOOK CARE OF me, showed me a different kind of love than Brick ever had. His presence made it easy for me to forget Brick.

Eight months into my relationship with Tigga, my best friend Zephoria started getting really sick. It began with her daughter. At 3 years old, Zephoria's daughter, Zaria, was still in diapers and unable to walk or talk. Having an older son, Zephoria knew this was abnormal behavior and took her to the doctor to get checked out. The doctors reviewed Zaria symptoms and behaviors and suggested that Zaria may have HIV. They tested her and sure enough, Zaria's test results revealed that at the age of 3, her tiny body was battling full blown AIDS.

"If she got it, I know I got it. They think she was born with it," Zephoria told me. At this time, the HIV/AIDS epidemic was growing and there wasn't much research to treat or prevent it. Zephoria knew it was just a matter of time before her symptoms began to show and decided she needed to get tested. I could see the shame and sadness in Zephoria's face as she discussed Zaria's results and the possibility of her also being positive. I was at a loss on what to do, but I knew that no matter what, I would be there for her.

"Well, I heard you can still live a long healthy life with it and I'm gonna still love you and treat you the same regardless," I reassured her. "Whatever you need, I got you."

Shortly after Zaria's diagnosis, Zephoria suffered a stroke. She knew Zaria's condition was too far gone for her to ever get better. The anxiety of losing her child and the question of her having HIV or AIDS herself completely overwhelmed her. Zephoria was admitted to the hospital after the stroke and tested immediately.

Zephoria never actually told me the results of her test. She was discharged and put on bed rest with an in-home nurse shortly after the stroke. Whether she told me her results or not, I knew my best friend was dying and it was harder on me than I would've ever expected. We were only 26. It felt like life was just getting started for us.

My own anxiety started kicking in and at the time, I could not explain what I was feeling. I was visiting Zephoria daily and everyday I watched her get weaker and weaker. I watched as hope left her eyes and the silly, laughing friend I once knew became depressed and withdrawn. Life slowly drained out of her and it hurt me to watch her struggle. I would often sit with her and rub her hands, her forehead and her feet while she would just lay in my lap and cry. Most of the time, we didn't even talk. I just sat there quietly and held space for her the same way I would for my mother as a little girl.

After a while, I needed confirmation of Zephoria's diagnosis. It just bothered me that I didn't really know what was wrong with my friend. I asked about the test results, and I was often brushed off by her or her mom. At one point, she tried to tell me that she had Sickle

Cell, but I had a strong feeling that wasn't true. Since I knew about Zaria, I was hurt that she didn't trust me with the obvious truth, so I went to find out for myself. One day while the nurse was giving Zephoria a bath, I went into her file and read the diagnosis. It confirmed that Zephoria did in fact have full-blown AIDS.

It felt like I was constantly losing people I loved. So much of sitting with Zephoria triggered memories of the time I spent with my mother in her final days. I didn't know how to balance that emotional trigger of losing my mother, being there for my best friend, working, and looking after Shosh. I knew it wasn't about me, but the tug of depression was strong.

Tigga saw that I was struggling and told me that I could stop working and see about my friend. "I'll take care of you. Go take care of her," he said one evening while I was telling him about my day with Zephoria. I immediately took him up on his offer and quit my job the next day.

After I quit my job, I sat with Zephoria from 9am to 5pm everyday like a full time job. I would drop Shosh off at daycare and I would get to Zephoria's house right as her mother was leaving for work. Zephoria's mother was a deputy sheriff and stayed with her overnight, so someone needed to be with Zephoria during the day and I gladly took on that role. While I sat with Zephoria daily, Tigga took care of everything at home like he said he would.

I couldn't tell you how long I sat with Zephoria. I continued to be there as she grew weaker. I wanted so badly to make her smile the way she used to. I wanted so badly to hear her yell "Summmmer Heeeeat" the way she did when we were just 13. I didn't know that I was already grieving. One day I got her to dress up and dragged her to the mall to take pictures like we did when we were younger. I knew the photos could be our last, but I wanted her to feel some type of joy again.

Zephoria decided that she wanted to be married before she died. So, three months before she died, her mom paid for a wedding and she married her boyfriend.

When Zephoria passed, I didn't know what to do with myself. My outlook on life shifted completely. I became curious about death and began to wonder about my own mortality as well as Shoshanna's. Tigga continued to take care of things and told me I didn't have to go back to work if I didn't want to. So, I decided to volunteer at Grady Hospital with AIDS patients. There was a part of me that was still hurt that Zephoria died without telling me that she had AIDS and I wanted her to look down on me from heaven and see that she had nothing to be ashamed of with me. I would've always had her back.

Zephoria's death changed me. I really wanted to understand death at the time and decided to enroll in mortuary school. I spoke to Tigga about it and as always, he was encouraging and prepared to foot the bill. He sent me to school full-time and paid cash for it. For the next two years, I would take Shosh to daycare, go to school until noon and then volunteer at Grady until 5.

At this point, it had been a couple years since I last spoke to Brick. My relationship with my father had improved drastically. He saw that I was doing well in school and volunteering at a hospital. He offered to help me get through school without having to worry about bills and other expenses. He knew I was in debt from being with Brick and gave me $10,000 to pay off all my bills while I was in school.

I graduated from mortuary school with perfect attendance in two years and received my Associate's Degree. At one point, calculus and chemistry kicked my ass and I found myself in danger of being kicked out, but I pushed on. I was so proud of myself. It felt good to have everyone proud of me after dealing with the loss of my best friend. I wanted so badly for my dad to see me do something special after everything that had happened between us. I could not allow failure to be an option.

Once I graduated from mortuary school, I started working part-time with my cousin at his funeral home. The pay was trash, but I enjoyed the experience of dressing up and driving the limo at funerals.

Working with family at the funeral home was a mess. Sometimes I would get paid, sometimes I would not. Since I was part-time, I was last on the totem pole whenever money was tight. "We can't pay you today, but we'll try to double up on your next check," was a phrase I started to hear a bit too much.

~ ~ ~

"Hehehe!"

Yarrow's deep, breathy laugh grossed me out every time.

"STOP!" I yelled and swatted his hand away from my behind as I got out of the car.

"Hehehe!" he continued.

Working at the mortuary became another moment in my life that I didn't realize how serious the situation I was in actually was. Yarrow was my older cousin who owned the mortuary with his wife Lavender. He was a well-dressed older man, who's money and style attracted a lot of women to him. It made his wife bitter and jealous of every woman around, and made him feel like he could say and do what he wanted to any woman.

As they aged, their daughter-in-law, Zinnia, ran everything. Yarrow's son, YAP, had no interest in running the family business and Zinnia, a graduate of mortuary school herself, took over.

Yarrow was a creep. Because they let Zinnia do whatever she wanted, I often found myself stuck running tedious errands with him. Whenever I needed to pick up a death certificate or a body, Yarrow would be the one to take me. I absolutely hated riding around with him. Yarrow had a habit of pinching or rubbing my butt as I would get out of the car whenever we had to go grab something while riding around. I would yell at him to stop and he would just laugh that deep breathy laugh that I had grown to absolutely hate. It's like it didn't even faze him that he was inappropriately touching his little cousin!

Yarrow acted like it was a cute joke between us. It got to the point that even when we were in the office and Zinnia had to run out, he'd find a way to come to my desk and rub his hand between my legs. Whenever I'd yell stop, he'd give me that same creepy laugh and walk away with an unlit cigar in his mouth. I would just sit there shaking my head like, ugh…

Even though I was an adult, it still didn't occur to me that Yarrow was sexually harassing me and that I had the power to make him stop. All I knew was to say stop in the moment and swing at him. In hindsight, I should have said something. I didn't even tell Tigga what was happening.

His wife Lavender was mean as a rattle snake, but Zinnia, his daughter-in-law, would have most likely helped me figure things out. Instead of saying something, I did the only thing I knew how when I felt violated, I fought back. Because he was older, I would punch him one time to get him to leave me alone. It would always work for the moment, but he would still come back and try again. In my mind, I was not being abused or a victim because I fought back. I always fought back.

Although I liked making my own money, as little as it was, I told Tigga that I couldn't work for Yarrow anymore. I told him about the missing paychecks but avoided the part about Yarrow harassing me. I knew Tigga would have had his body sent to the Everglades. At that time in my life, I believed I was handling it.

Tigga was supportive as always. He encouraged me to walk away from the mortuary and reassured me that he would continue to take care of me and Shosh... and he did.

Chapter Thirteen

8.5 Years

...You know that when your faith is tested, your endurance has a chance to grow. So let it grow, for when your endurance is fully developed, you will be perfect and complete, needing nothing.
-James 1: 3-4

Shortly after quitting the job at the mortuary, I started applying for other jobs. I landed a 3-day administrative job with an internet service provider through a temp agency. I did so well at that job that I was invited back week after week until I was hired on completely. I ended up working for the company 8 years.

In those 8 years, my life completely changed. Shosh and Tigga had become so close that she asked him to be her daddy. Tigga immediately stepped up as Shosh's father and he began to be known as "good daddy" while Brick became known as "bad daddy." Tigga, Shosh, and I operated like a family unit and Brick couldn't be farther from that picture. We were doing really well.

At this point, I was 28 years old and making 60K per year at the internet company--the most money I had ever made working a full-time job. Between my salary and Tigga's money, I became naive about the value of money. I was just as frivolous as I wanted to be until folks around me started talking to me about buying a house.

I prepared to buy my first house in a brand new subdivision in Covington, Georgia. Three bedrooms, two baths, a two car garage, and a full acre of land. I was so proud to have a real home for Shosh and myself until I was met with a rude awakening.

"Summer… are you married?" My closing attorney asked as she shuffled through my closing paperwork.

"Yes, but we haven't been together in years." I responded.

"Well, I have some bad news for you…" Her voice trailed. "If you don't get a legal divorce, your husband will have full rights to your home. That's Georgia law. So... If you don't plan on having anything to do with him going forward, I would advise you to officially file for divorce so that he can not claim this home."

I was stunned. I had just been living my life all this time and not even thinking about my marriage to Brick and how it could affect my process of moving on. I hadn't had any communication with Brick in years. Since I was only 17 when we married, I really had no idea how our marriage would affect me in the future.

I closed on my house successfully, but I wasted no time filing for a divorce. The last thing I needed was for Brick to find out I bought a house and then pop up and complicate things. Tigga and I had gotten too comfortable with the fact that we were both married to other people, but in love with each other. This was exactly the push I needed to stop ignoring the fact that I was still legally married to Brick and file for a divorce.

~ ~ ~

Brick was nowhere to be found when it was time for him to show up in court. I knew he didn't like to deal with the law, but I had hoped he'd at least show up to get this over with. I ended up having to wait until he failed to appear after being subpoenaed to move forward with the divorce. Because of his antics, it took about 6 months for Brick and I to be officially divorced.

Shortly after settling into my new house, I purchased a customized Eddie Bauer expedition. Life was good. Tigga continued to take care of me, but with my salary at the internet company, I was proud that I was able to take care of myself and Shosh as well. If he chose to abandon me tomorrow, I knew I would still be okay.

The family unit we created worked well for Shosh and I. However, after I divorced Brick, a part of me expected Tigga to move towards divorcing his wife as well. Instead, Tigga continued to mind two households with ease. I knew he was unhappy at home with his wife, but he seemed to truly enjoy being a family man with both families. He would go to all of Shosh's school events while providing food and equipment to his son's football team as a booster parent. He was a good father.

Because Tigga was able to take care of both households, I found myself conflicted. After being with Brick, I had vowed that I would never put another woman through what he put me through. At the same time, Brick, unlike Tigga, didn't have anything to offer any of the women in his life. I told myself that as long as Tigga was caring for us and his other family with ease, it was a win-win for everyone.

Tigga loved playing daddy to Shosh. He wanted her to be as much a part of his family as his other children and made that known to his family. In order to bring us around without questions, Tigga concocted a whole story about how he had momentarily stepped out on his wife and got another woman (me) pregnant. I, "the baby mama," had just decided to tell him about his daughter.

We boldly kept this story going for almost nine years. Everyone accepted Shoshanna as his biological daughter. Since he already had two sons, Tigga's family respected how much Tigga adored and spoiled "his daughter." His wife, his two older sons, and even his parents accepted Shoshanna and I as their extended family. Tigga had a way about him that left them no choice.

To this day, I can't believe how bold we were in getting his family to believe our story so that we could be together publicly. I mean... I was dating this man and around his immediate family and parents with the pretense that Shosh was his biological daughter like it was no big deal.

~ ~ ~

"You gotta take care of my daughter."

"Yea, but pleading guilty is gonna take you away from us for five years. We been through that before." I looked Tigga in his eyes. This love was so different from what I experienced with Brick and the thought of losing Tigga frightened me. The whole scenario felt all too familiar and I could feel the anxiety swell up in my chest. I felt safe with Tigga around and the thought of him going to prison for five years was like dead weight on my shoulders.

"I know, but you know I'll take care of y'all like I always do. Ain't nothing to worry about. And, if I turn myself in they won't bother with you," Tigga responded.

He was right.

"Well, what about your wife?" I asked. "I feel like she's gonna have more access to you than me when they lock you up and she ain't gonna look out for you the way I will. I think we should be the ones married."

"I can't do what you really asking me to do right now, Summer. I told you that already. I'll give you a power of attorney to handle anything you need to. I just need you to stick by me through this."

I sat down on the couch. Defeated. He

was still a married man and even though I knew he would find a way to take care of us while he was locked up, I wanted to be the one married to him.

"Aight then… you stuck by me all this time, so I got you. Me and Shosh will be here."

Tigga walked over to the couch and kissed me on my forehead.

"Thank you my Summer Heat," he smiled.

The feds had been watching Tigga the entire time we were together. He was so smooth with his business that it took them five years to build a case on him. Even still, the police struggled to get any real evidence on him and ended up only being able to get him on conspiracy.

When they implicated me as one of his people in the investigation, Tigga did not hesitate to take the plea deal to protect me and Shosh. I'll admit. I did some work for him. Shosh and I were reaping the benefits of his lifestyle, so to me, it didn't hurt to do a couple runs for him every now and then. I started making drops and dealing with the money when he needed an extra set of hands. He knew I could handle it, but he was always adamant about not wanting to get me too involved.

I took Tigga's sentencing hard. The people I loved were always leaving me in some way and it wore on me. I started to feel like if we didn't get married, I would lose him forever.

~ ~ ~

"Tigga, just divorce her. I bet she ain't even been up there to see you yet," I told Tigga on his first call from prison.

"Heat, that's not the move right now. Be patient. I told you I will take care of you. Why you worried about that?"

"I don't understand, Tigga. Sh--"

"Heat, I didn't call to argue with you behind this," Tigga cut me off. "I'll do my time by myself if you just trying to get on the phone and argue."

"Oh! OK cool!" I hollered into the phone and hung up.

I was livid. Tigga called me from prison and all I could think about was him divorcing his wife and marrying me. At this point I had been divorced for a minute and did not understand why he couldn't just move on like I did. We argued the entire time during our first conversation and when I hung up, that was it. If he didn't call me, I knew that was it because I couldn't call him.

~ ~ ~

"You need to stop being so selfish and take my grandbaby up there to see her father!" Tigga's mother hollered into the phone.

"I don't have money to be buying plane tickets to Pennsylvania. I didn't tell him to go up there." I hollered back.

"I don't know why you don't have the money. You should be able to afford that. I know my son has taken good care of his daughter and of you."

She struck a nerve with that one. Tigga's mother and I had been going back and forth for weeks about taking Shosh to see Tigga. I entertained it at first, but now I was over it. She wasn't about to worry me to death about the situation. The reality was, Tigga made the decision to be sent to the federal prison in Pennsylvania while his son was enrolled at Penn State. He wanted to be close to his son, so that his son would be able to visit him often. The down side was that his decision meant that he was too far for casual visits from Shosh and I. And, since he didn't want to marry me, I was angry with him.

"THAT AIN'T EVEN HER REAL DADDY!!!! STOP CALLING ME AND HARASSING ME! I'M NOT GOING UP THERE!! SHOSHANNA AIN'T EVEN HIS DAUGHTER!!!" I shouted back at her.

Click

I hung up and plopped down on my couch. I couldn't believe I just blew our cover. I was so drained in my hurt that all I wanted was for everyone to hurt just like I was hurting.

The next morning Tigga called. I was excited to hear from him but fought not to let it show. I knew he was calling about what I said to his mother.

"You told my mama Shosh wasn't mine?" He asked quietly.

"Damn you sound like you didn't already know that," I laughed nervously.

"Well I take care of her like she's mine, so I'm trying to figure out why you would say that. She is mine."

"Your mama was getting on my nerves, harassing me to bring Shosh up there. I don't have money for all that."

"I figured. Well, she didn't believe it anyway. She thinks you are just trying to make her mad so she will leave you alone."

"Well shit, that too," I responded.

Tigga was mad but since his mother didn't believe it, he let it go. It was crazy to me that we had pulled off the story of Shosh being his daughter so well for so long, that the truth didn't even seem believable anymore.

After about a year without Tigga, I found myself struggling financially. I never really had the need to budget, so I just kept spending like I always did.

I was single again, so I started hanging. I continued to make good money at the internet company, but it still wasn't the cash flow I was used to. Not to mention, I was starting to feel lonely.

One afternoon I was getting ready to leave the office for the day when I was stopped by a colleague.

"Summer Heat?" A deep voice behind me said. Startled, I turned around and saw one of the building maintenance men standing behind me. I had seen him around a few times, but as long as I worked there, we never really had a conversation.

"Yes! How you know my name?" I asked.

"Who doesn't know your name?" He laughed. "You're popular around here, so I wanted to introduce myself. I'm Suri."

"Sorry?"

"Suri." He corrected me. Little did I know, I had his name right the first time.

Suri and I hit it off. He was cool. I was never 100% sure of his role with the company, but I enjoyed meeting him before work and for lunch. When he told me he was single with no kids, I was amazed. After being in the relationships I had been in since high school, it felt good to meet someone that didn't have the baggage and family ties that I was used to. I welcomed him into my life with open arms.

Suri was a cool guy, but there was still something that was slightly off about him. He felt too good to be true. I had been through enough in life at this point to know that I couldn't ignore my gut.

One day, I decided to carry out my own little investigation on Mr. Perfect. Lo and behold, I find out that this man is married with three children. Not only is he married, but he has a twin brother who actually is single. This man had been telling me about his brother's life as if it were his this whole time! Worse yet, I realized that he had already planned to deny knowing me if I were to ever see him out with his family and then be able to tell his wife that I was confusing him with his brother. The balls!! He thought he had his whole game figured out, but all I could think was, no one plays me!

One morning I called like I always did.

"Where are you?" He asked.

"Look Outside," I responded.

I was parked behind his car, blocking it in. When he saw me at his house, he freaked out.

"Meet me at the job!"

I headed to the job to wait for him to meet me there. I backed my Expedition into my parking space and waited for him to pull in. A few minutes later, I watched him as he parked and walked toward my car. I could tell he was angry.

"What the fuck were you doing at my house?" Suri yelled as he swung open my car door and got in my face. Clearly not the reaction of a single man.

Immediately, I moved my hand in the direction of my .45. I had never seen Suri this mad. I couldn't understand how it was that men could do wrong, and then get violently upset when their lies were exposed. I was in disbelief.

Somewhere in between him yelling and pointing in my face, Suri grabbed my arm. Instinctively, I reached for the .45 Ruger, took off the safety, and held the barrel to his mouth.

"LET. ME. GO." I demanded.

"Shit. Wow. OK," Suri said as he let go of my arm and backed up. He slammed my door in and started pounding on the hood of my truck. I jumped out of the truck, put my safety back on, and hit him in the back of his head.

"Fuck you! Stupid ass bitch, you hit me!" Suri yelled walking backwards towards the building.

"Yea! You lying ass country mutha fucker!" I screamed, feeling the heat of tears I knew were about to come.

Suri ran over to the parking lot elevator. As soon as he was out of sight, I went back to my truck and cried. I was so hurt. I couldn't bear the thought of losing someone I cared about again. I was really starting to like him.

I got myself together and went into the building as if nothing happened.

"Good Morning!" I greeted everyone as I walked in. After 8 years, you get to know everybody. Immediately, I walked over to Gladys and Luna's desk.

"I gotta tell y'all what just happened to me," I whispered.

"What Sis???" Gladys responded.

"Summer Heat, can you come in here for a moment?" I heard my supervisor say as I prepared to tell Gladys and Luna the story.

"Sure!" I responded. My supervisor was such a handsome and charismatic dude that I loved going into his office to chat. Today, however, it felt different.

"Good Morning," he stated as I sat across from him. "We just got a call from Human Resources. You need to report to their meeting room now."

I looked at him surprised. My performance at work had always been pretty good, so I couldn't see what HR would want with me. I got up and walked towards the conference room.

On my way down the hall, I spotted Suri sitting on the other side of the HR office in tears.

"OH HELL NAW!!" I thought to myself. I couldn't believe this fool went crying to HR knowing our business had nothing to do with work. I walked into the conference room. There were three people from HR already seated and waiting for me.

"Summer, can you tell us what happened this morning?"

"Not much, I just walked in a few minutes ago. I haven't really had the chance to sit down at my desk yet."

"Before you came in today, Summer."

I was already annoyed. "Wouldn't that be personal?" I responded.

"Well, we have a report of you stalking a colleague and then pulling a gun on said colleague in the Parking Lot this morning."

"Stalking? I wasn't stalking him! Suri told me he was a single man, we started dating, and then I found out he lied and had a whole family! Then, when I got ready to ask him about it, he grabbed me!" I was livid as I gave my side of the story to HR. I was in disbelief that he would bring our job into this.

"If you were concerned about Suri's motives for dating you, you should have reported him. But since he reported you, we have to investigate his claim. You are suspended until the investigation is complete."

I could not believe this was happening. I left the conference room, went to my desk, and packed a few of my things. Two weeks later I was contacted by HR. They found evidence of the altercation in the parking lot and I was given the option to resign or be terminated. I chose to resign.

With no job, and no Tigga, it was only a matter of time before that spending caught up to me and I was back at square one. It wouldn't be long before this whole ordeal would cost me everything.

Chapter Fourteen

Rock

...And trials, for we know that they help us develop endurance... And endurance develops strength of character, and character strengthens our confident hope of salvation... And this hope will not lead to disappointment.

-Romans 5: 3-5

I ENDED UP OUT OF WORK FOR three months. I tried to juggle my house note and car note for as long I could so I wouldn't have to move back in with Reign. I knew she would have no problem letting Shosh and I stay with her, but I wanted that to be my last resort.

The bills continued to grow and I just

couldn't keep my head above water. I finally landed a job as a paraprofessional at a local school that paid less than half of what I was making at the Internet company. The job helped me to have some money, but it was nowhere close to what I needed to sustain the life I had built. I was stressed out and barely making ends meet by the time my hairstylist offered me a solution.

"Heat!" I looked up and saw Diamond, my stylist, standing in front of me at the grocery store.

"Hey Diamond!" I said and leaned in for a hug.

"Girl how you been? When you coming back to the shop?" She asked.

"Man..." I started. "I actually lost my job, so I kinda put that on the back burner for now. I'm just trying to take care of my house note and car note right now."

I was honest with her because I figured, what else did I have to lose? Shit happened to everyone right? This was mine.

"Damn Heat, I'm sorry to hear that. You know, my husband and I just got into Real Estate. We might be able to help you with your house until you get back on your feet."

"Really?" I was intrigued. I felt desperate to find a solution to this mess I found myself in.

"Yea, let's meet up next week with my husband and talk about it," Diamond responded. I agreed and we set up a meeting at my house the following Monday evening.

Diamond and her husband, Coop, came over Monday night to discuss how they could help me save my house while I got my finances together. They proposed that I rent my home out and let the renters cover the mortgage payments.

"We will pretty much act like property managers or landlords on your behalf. We already have a renter that we can move into the home for you," Diamond stated.

"That's Right! We are ready to go! We don't even have to waste time looking for someone," Coop co-signed.

"OK! So, what do I need to do?" I asked, ready to get on board. It seemed like a win-win situation for everyone. I was thinking I could stay with Reign while Diamond and Coop rented out my house to make sure the mortgage got paid. It seemed simple enough.

Coop pulled out a folder with a stack of papers. "All you'll have to do is complete this paperwork that we've prepared for you. This top sheet is your current contact info and the address of where you will be moving to. The second sheet is a Quitclaim Deed. That just gives us the permission to act on your behalf as owners," he stated.

I looked over the papers. I wasn't exactly sure what he was talking about or what the Quitclaim Deed was about, but I knew my mortgage would get paid and that was my priority. I signed and completed the paperwork on the spot.

A few weeks after our meeting, Shosh and I moved out of our home and back in with my sister Reign. Diamond and Coop went through the process of securing the deed to my house and began renting it out.

I had no idea that I had just signed away my house.

~ ~ ~

My salary as a teacher's assistant was trash. I barely made $18,000 a year. I started looking for a part-time job with Gladys, my best friend from the internet company. We found a part-time job doing taxes and, in no time, we became the fun girls in the office. We started making extra tips on the side or be personally requested by clients.

As much as I enjoyed my part-time job, I still struggled to keep my head above water. I struggled to keep up with my car payments and my beloved Eddie Bauer expedition ended up getting repossessed. I had now lost my house and my car.

I was so angry that I had found myself in this position. I couldn't blame anyone but myself, but at the same time I also couldn't help but think: Why didn't that fool just tell me the truth about his life? Why did he have to grab me? He lied to me to cheat on his wife and children, and yet here I was picking up the pieces of the fall out months later while he was probably comfortably at home with his wife. I was hurt and embarrassed in ways I couldn't even describe.

One afternoon, I was sitting in the tax office when a man walked in and sat at my desk. I looked up and there was Rock, an old friend I dated in High School, sitting at my desk.

"Rock! What's up?? What you doing here?" I asked.

I hadn't seen Rock in years. I remembered that he was a great football player, but got caught up in the drug game at a young age. He ended up dropping out of school to move major weight with his brothers. With everything that I was going through, it was exciting to see him.

"Man, I can't call it. I need my taxes done and I happened to stop here. When I saw you, I was like bet! I know her! She could do my taxes!" He laughed. He sounded so different. So mature. He was still handsome, smelling goooo-O-oooood and built like a football player and Eddie Levert wrapped all in one. I felt the feelings I once had for him start to resurface instantly.

"OK! I got you! Here is what I need for you to fill out," I responded and handed him our company paperwork. As we reviewed his information, I noticed that he had a little money and a stable job. He was definitely not the kid I knew from high school and that intrigued me a lot. After having two significant men in my life get locked up, I was ready to meet someone who was on the straight and narrow.

"Thanks, Heat! You a lifesaver. So what you been doing? We need to catch up!" He stated as he stood up to leave.

"Yea we do! Take my number."

We exchanged numbers and he left. I found myself all giddy and excited. After all the BS I had just been through, I figured Rock would be a safe catch from my past. I knew his history, so I assumed I knew enough of him already to not have to deal with a bunch of lies again.

The following day, Rock called and we ended up going out to eat. I learned that he was now a little league football coach who had become popular in his community. It felt good to share memories with someone familiar who seemed to be out doing good in the world. We started hanging out regularly and I felt myself catching feelings. Soon enough, I introduced him to Shosh and he introduced me to his two sons. I knew he also had a daughter back when we were in high school and she was now living with her mother. After dealing with Suri, I felt a sense of comfort knowing that Rock was honest about his three kids and was an active father in their lives.

A month into our rekindled, but now adult, relationship, Rock proposed. I hadn't spoken to Tigga in nearly a year so it felt good to be wanted again by someone I felt like I could trust. So, I accepted.

"Shosh, you like Rock?"

"Yea, he fun," Shosh responded while getting herself a snack from the fridge.

"OK good! We gonna get married," I stated, relieved that she liked him.

"Oh! Wait Mama, I don't like him that much! Not to marry him! Don't marry him Mama! What about good daddy? You still mad at him?" Shosh looked at me wide-eyed. I was thrown off. I did not expect that reaction from her.

"Shosh, Tigga still in jail and I'm grown. I do what I want to do. You don't tell me what to do. You need to stay in a child's place. All I asked you was if you liked him." Shosh frowned and walked off. To this day, I wish I didn't dismiss her feelings like that.

Rock and I got married shortly after the proposal. His father, who was a preacher, counseled and married us. After we got married, we rented a five bedroom house from the teacher I worked with and moved our family in--my daughter and his two sons. His older daughter would come and visit every now and then as well. It felt good to have a family again. Everything felt almost perfect.

Every now and then I would go to Rock's little league games on Saturdays. I continued to work part-time preparing taxes, so most Saturdays I was either working or doing something with Shosh. One particular Saturday, he had a big game that I wanted to show up and support him at. The game was already packed by the time I got there, so I went over to him to say hello and let him know I was there. We hugged and I went to find a seat with Shosh. After I found a seat off to the side, I started looking around just to take it all in.

Rock was in and out the crowd mixing and mingling with everyone. The more I watched him move, the more it looked like he forgot that I was there. Women seemed to come from everywhere. Everytime I looked up there was a different woman in his face, and he was right back in theirs. I called Gladys to meet me at the game to witness what I was seeing. She popped up and confirmed that his interactions with these women seemed like more than just the mothers of his players, or members of the audience. They seemed to be women that he had intimate relationships with. Watching him move was like I was watching someone I didn't know. All I could think was, what the hell did I get myself into… again.

That night when Rock came home, I went off.

"Rock, did you forget I came to see you today?" I asked.

"What? N-No! I knew you were at the game" He responded. I knew immediately he was lying. I was sure he forgot that I was there. I don't usually attend his games and based on what I saw that day, I could tell he was used to moving like a single man when I wasn't around.

"It seem like you made time to entertain every woman at that game you could. Every time I looked at you it was another female in your face and you were right back in theirs."

"Heat, those just my friends. I'm a coach.

I coach their sons. What you expect?"

"Your friends? So why I don't know them? They looked like more than friends. Don't play me. I didn't even recognize you today. I feel like I don't even know who you are. All these damn women you dealing with and I don't know a single one of them," I responded.

We argued back and forth for a while before going to bed. I was livid. Here it was, I thought this was about to be the perfect solution to my messy life, and it was starting to look like he was on the same shit as everyone else. I felt like I couldn't catch a break.

The next morning Rock left and was gone for a long while. Now that my peace had been disturbed, the blinders were off and I knew there had to be more to what he had going on. I walked into the closet in our bedroom and started poking around. A briefcase propped up against the wall, hit the floor and opened up. Papers were everywhere. At first, I looked down at the closet floor angry that I would have to clean up the stack of papers that fell out until I noticed that there was also a set of photos that fell out.

"What the fuck?" I said to myself as I looked over pics of several different children at different ages. I picked up a few of the photographs, flipped them over, and read the messages on the back.

To my Daddy....

To Daddy...

To Dad...

Daddy? I picked up photo after photo of different children outside of his two sons and daughter. I couldn't believe that I had been lied to to this extent again. It felt like I was living in the twilight zone. I took the photos and I spread them out on the bed for whenever Rock decided to come back home.

"Why you go through my stuff?" Rock asked as soon as he walked in the room.

"Why I go through your stuff?? Rock, you worried about the wrong thing. Who the fuck are these people? How many kids you got? All these say daddy!!" I responded

"Those not my kids! They my brother's kids. I'm holding his pictures for him, so his girl don't find out he got outside kids." The story sounded believable and questionable all at the same time. If he was okay hiding kids for his brother, then he definitely wouldn't have a problem hiding them for himself.

"I'm not a fool! These also got your name on it!" I yelled.

"You trippin'! Why would you go through my shit anyway? Do I go through your shit?" Rock responded. I could tell he was about to make it about me going through his stuff and try to avoid talking about what I found. At that moment, I knew I would have to do my own research on what he really had going on. He was never going to tell me the truth on his own.

I did some digging and found out that this man actually had TEN KIDS! Ten! I kept the pictures and when he left his sons at home with me, I would show them a picture and say, "Look at your brother's / sister's picture that I found." And of course, Lil' Rock would confirm every single photo to be a picture of one of his siblings. His sons knew about his other children. I was the only one that didn't. I couldn't believe this shit was happening to me again.

That night Rock left and didn't come back until the next morning. In my mind, once you disrespected the sun, you disrespected me. And, I was tired of being disrespected.

I sat upstairs in our bedroom waiting to hear him pull up. As soon as I heard his car pull into the driveway, I got my trusty .45, sat on the bed and sat the gun on the bed next to me. I didn't plan to use it, or even touch it. I just wanted him to know he had the wrong one.

The anxiety rose in my chest as I heard him walking up the stairs. He opened the bedroom door and looked straight over at me sitting on the bed.

"What the fuck Heat? You still on this shit? I know you ain't pull no fucking gun out on me!" He yelled.

At this point, I hadn't said a word yet. "Sir, I didn't pull no gun out on you," I responded in a calm voice. "It just so happened to be laying on the bed. I just need you to know that when you disrespect the sun, you are disrespecting me. You didn't even try to fix this, you just ran to the next woman that would let you lay up in their bed all night. So guess what? I can't do this."

"Can't do what Heat? I could've been at my boy's house. Why it always gotta be a woman? I got my sons in the house and shit and you over here trying to threaten my life."

"That don't help your case, Rock. And, did you see me touch the gun?" I asked calmly.

"Man, fuck you." Rock walked out the room, went downstairs, and called the police from the kitchen. I sat on the bed feeling like I was in the twilight zone again. These men lie, get caught, get mad, and then when you match their energy, they wanna gaslight you and play victim. This couldn't be happening. Not again.

Twenty minutes later, the police showed up. After we explained the situation, the female cop pulled me aside.

"Ma'am, I'm going to suggest that you

leave the house for a few hours. But, let me be real with you. I can look at y'all and tell you this ain't the type of guy you need to be with. He ain't worth you ending up in jail behind. I don't usually tell nobody to leave their husband, but I need you to pack your stuff and make a clean break from this. You got kids?"

"Yes, one daughter."

"Just one? Yea, this ain't for you. You can do better for you and your daughter."

She was right. We talked for nearly an hour and I took heed to her every word. I was grateful that she chose to minister to me instead of criminalizing me. At that moment, she recognized that I was a woman who was deeply hurt and not someone who meant to do anyone harm.

Following the officer's advice, I packed a few things for Shosh and I and left. I decided to go to my God-sister Sheree's house for the weekend. I felt bad for having to ask her to stay since she was already hosting family escaping Hurricane Katrina, but she lived the closest. The family welcomed Shosh and I over for the weekend with open arms.

When I got to my Sheree's house that Friday evening, I refused to take any of Rock's calls. Sheree was dating Rock's brother at the time. A part of me knew that he would tell Rock where I was, and a part of me hoped that he'd just keep it to himself.

That Sunday morning, Rock showed up. I was in the shower getting ready to go back home and I was thinking about him having an attitude when I got home because I ignored him. Suddenly, I heard the muffled sounds of commotion downstairs.

"Where Heat?"

"She's in the shower Rock, damn why you coming in here with all that?" Sheree yelled.

Before I could even process what was going on, the bathroom door swung open. Rock pushed his way into the bathroom, snatched the curtain down, and pulled me out of the shower by my hair. Rock dragged me down the stairs cussing while I screamed for him to let me go. I was so embarrassed. Everyone was watching and yelling for him to stop.

"Nigga! Yo! What are you doing? Let her go!" I heard someone yell. At that moment, Rock let me go and I ran back upstairs. I heard more commotion downstairs while I hurried and got myself dressed and ready to leave. As angry as I was, I didn't even cry. It was almost like I couldn't cry. I just stood there feeling lost. I didn't come out of the bathroom until it quieted down. I walked out of the bathroom, and down the stairs to the living room. Embarrassed. Rock was gone.

"You okay?" Sheree's Aunt asked.

"I'm good. Where's Shosh? We gotta go." I responded casually. I was trying to hide my embarrassment with everything in me.

I turned around and saw Shosh and my niece, Korena, looking on with fear and tears in their eyes. I hated seeing my daughter like that. The police were immediately called. After they took my report and left, I had to go.

I thanked Sheree and gave out a few goodbye hugs. I was fighting back tears and trying to appear nonchalant about the whole thing, but I was so deeply hurt and humiliated. I knew I pissed Rock off by ignoring him all weekend, but I never expected him to show up and handle me like that in front of everyone. Flashbacks of Brick beating me on his mother's lawn danced in my head and I felt sick to my stomach.

Our relationship was definitely over for me at that point. Not only was I embarrassed, but I felt horrible for bringing that drama into Sheree's house. Seeing the look on Shosh and Korena's face was enough to let me know that something had to give. I walked outside, got Shosh and went home.

When I got home, Rock nor his sons were there. I walked into the house and saw that he had moved all their stuff out. He was the breadwinner, and knew I couldn't pay the rent alone. I was still working as a para at the school and working part time at the tax office--barely making $22,000 a year.

I ended up having to write up an early termination for our lease. The teacher that I was working with, who was also my landlord, was pissed. Even though I told her everything that had happened, she still took me to court and sued me for breaking the lease. I was livid at the position I was in yet again because a man chose to lie to me. At this point, we had barely been married a month and I was in total disbelief about how much had been uncovered in such a short length of time. I filed an annulment and got myself a lawyer.

"You're going to need to reverse the annulment, Heat. You've gotta divorce him instead so you can get alimony to pay for the lawsuit," my lawyer told me as we sat in her office.

"We weren't married that long." I responded.

"You were married to him long enough for him to change your lifestyle. You can get alimony for that. He really can't leave you hanging like that." She advised me.

I did exactly as she said. I reversed the annulment and filed for divorce.

When we finally got to court, I told the judge everything, from how we met, to the women at the game, to the photos in the closet, to him dragging me down the stairs at my God-sister's house. The judge was appalled. My lawyer then added that I had been sued by my landlord for breaking my lease and was barely making $20,000 a year. The judge went off.

"OK, I've heard enough," The judge responded. He looked over at Rock. "You can't get married to somebody, decide to abandon your life, let them get sued for having to break the lease in a house you lived in with them and three children and think that that's OK. I'm awarding Summer Heat $10,000 in alimony."

"WHAT? I can't pay that!!" Rock shouted at the judge. "I got 10 kids to see about!"

"Oh! So now you got ten kids??" I shouted over at him as he continued to yell about his sudden responsibilities.

"Hey!" The judge banged his gavel and looked over at Rock. "That's enough. You will pay her $10,000 and if you say one more thing in my court, I'm gonna lock you up." The judge then looked over at me, "Ma'am, the next time you look for a husband, please don't find one that got 10 kids!"

I was so embarrassed that I couldn't even hold my head up to look at the judge. I fought back tears feeling like the biggest fool on the planet.

Chapter Fifteen

Tigga II

And remember that the heavenly Father to whom you pray has no favorites. He will judge or reward you according to what you do. So you must live in reverent fear of Him during your time here...
-1 Peter 1: 16-18

"What's going on with you, Heat? I talked to Reign and she couldn't tell me where you and Shosh lived." Tigga asked.

I found out that Tigga had still been communicating regularly with my sister. Reign had always helped me take care of Shosh, so I never questioned where she was getting the extra money from to buy things for her. It turned out that Tigga was mailing my sister child support checks for Shosh all this time. But, since we weren't speaking, he had no clue of how bad it really was.

"Yea, I'm kinda down on my luck right now. My money is tight. I lost the house… And then I lost the car." I was not about to tell him about the fool I married for a month.

"Damn, why didn't you tell me? OK, I'm gonna send you $1,000. I'll get the feds to send it as child support for my daughter."

A week later, a federal check labeled Child Support showed up in the mail. If there was one thing I knew about Tigga is that he kept his word and he took care of his people. I held on to the $1,000 to get a place for Shosh and I to stay. Before I even started looking, I ran into my other God-sister, Sasha, in the parking lot at Publix. We stood around and caught up for a while until I revealed to her that I needed a place for Shosh and I to stay. I had worn out my welcome with her brother footing hotel bills for Shosh and I and I really wanted a place of my own again.

To my surprise, Sasha's husband was a real estate investor with several rental properties. He had one newly renovated property that he had just evicted some people out of. Since it wasn't in the best area, he was uncomfortable with leaving it vacant too long. I told her that I didn't care where it was, I just needed a place for my daughter and I.

Within a few days, Sasha and her husband set everything up and Shosh and I moved into our new home right before Thanksgiving. Since it was the holidays, Sasha and her husband decided to bless us one more time and waived the rent until January. I was ecstatic. I was just starting to build a relationship with God and he was already coming through.

I still had the $1,000 from Tigga, so I called him to let him know what happened.

"Bet! Now take that money I gave you and get you a car instead. I'll contact my dealership and get things handled. All you'll have to do is take that power of attorney up there and that $1,000."

"OK." I responded. I knew he would make it happen.

A few weeks before Christmas, Tigga called me to let me know that everything was set up and I just had to go get the car. I went to the dealership with the check for $1,000 and the power of attorney. As promised, Tigga had a car reserved and ready for me to drive off in.

I walked into the dealership and walked over to the first person I saw.

"Summer Heat?" A voice said.

"Yes," I turned around and saw another car salesman standing there.

"Okay, I thought that was you. Tigga sent us a picture and told us you were coming in today."

I was caught off guard a bit. I couldn't believe this dude was really able to do all this from prison. We walked to the back of the lot and stopped in front of a clean, Black Lexus GS300.

"This is it." The salesman said pointing at the Lexus. "I just got some paperwork I need you to do and then you can just drive off."

"OK!" I replied, trying to conceal my excitement. I walked back to the office, went through the motions of buying a car, signed Tigga's name, handed them $1,000, and pulled off.

Just like that, Tigga made sure I had my life back. I even saw a change in Shosh when she realized good daddy and I were back on good terms. I realized that I really loved this man. He had been the most loyal of everyone I had been with. If he said it, it happened. If he loved you, he took care of you. It was that simple. He was a man with a big heart, and I loved him for it.

Tigga and I started speaking regularly again. At some point while he was in prison, his wife filed for divorce. "I should have left her when you told me to, but I was worried about my boys. You know I gotta make sure mine are good at all times," he confessed.

Tigga refused to go into details about what happened to make them finally get a divorce, but I was happy that the thought of us getting married when he came home felt more real.

"Look, when I get home, we are gonna work things out and everything will be like it should be."

"OK. We'll see," I responded, holding in my excitement. Despite all that had happened when he was away, it felt like everything was coming back around full circle.

The feds shipped Tigga to Alabama during his final year. That was an easy drive for Shosh and I to do from Georgia. We would hit I-20 every other weekend and drive to Alabama to visit him until he was released to transitional housing.

The day after Tigga moved into the half-way house he went back to work. I would pick him up and take him to and from work while he lived at the house. He was dead set on starting his own trucking company and wanted to pick up where he left off with the trucking company he was working with.

While Tigga was still at the half-way house, we got married and he was able to completely come home. Tigga moved in with me and Shosh and we returned to our lives as a family. Only this time, we really were a family.

I was so excited that it took me a long time to realize that those 5 years in prison changed Tigga in a way that I would never understand. I expected him to bounce back into the man he used to be and he just couldn't. As he settled back into his life, he began to resent God for allowing him to go to jail. He felt like he was a good person who always treated the folks he loved well and consequently, did not deserve to be the one caught up.

At this point, I had just started getting more into The Word, so I explained to him that God was like a real parent who sometimes has to rear his children for doing wrong. He may have been a great steward, but he was still a drug dealer. I tried to convince him that he had so much life left in him and still had an amazing support system of people who stuck by him, including Shosh and I. Tigga would listen to my attempts to cheer him up, but his wounds were deeper than I could mend. As time went on, he gradually became bitter.

Tigga coped with these emotions by throwing himself into work. He would work everyday of the week and it frustrated me. After all this time longing for him to return, he was still hardly around. I thought about my father and how he would work non-stop, leaving me lonely and raising myself. I refused to allow my husband to do the same thing to me. I enjoyed the comfort of a second income, but the truth was I wanted him more than the money.

The less Tigga gave me what I really needed from him, the more we argued. He was content with taking care of us financially--which I appreciated, but I wanted companionship. I wanted him to be there for me and all he wanted to do was work or sit around alone at the house. I know now that he was battling depression. At the time, I couldn't see it.

At times, he would be able to sense that I was getting antsy, and he would call and say, "Be ready when I get home, we going to dinner." That always excited me. We would go to beautiful restaurants and have really nice dinners that made me fall in love with him all over again. Other times, we would take Shosh down to the fair or just drive her to her friends' parties. I grew to love those moments intensely because of the quality time we shared as a couple and as a family, but the truth was... they were few and far between.

The arguing between Tigga and I intensified. Even though Tigga had no problem giving us his last, the feelings of loneliness and fear of sudden abandonment overwhelmed me everyday. Since he was already much older than me, he didn't care to hang out with my friends or seemed interested in the things I liked to do. He would just give me some money and send me out alone. It got to the point where my friends didn't even believe that I had a man who was taking care of me. That bothered me because I wanted them all to know that I had someone at home who loved me.

Despite everything we were going through, I remained faithful to Tigga because he had always taken care of me and Shosh. God began to show me that money wasn't everything and I had to admit to myself that as much as I loved this man, the relationship we had was no longer working for me. He wasn't the same man I knew before he was incarcerated.

Each day Tigga grew more and more distant and I started to wonder if he was taking care of a new woman and her child now that we were the ones married. The guilt started to eat me up and the constant arguing eventually escalated to physical. Once things started getting physical, I knew that we were not going to be able to make it work anymore.

Chapter Sixteen

The Beginning of the End

For the Mighty One is holy, and he has done great things for me. He shows mercy from generation to generation to all who fear him.

-Luke 1:49-51

"Momma. My daddy gone," Shosh said in a low, even tone.

"What?" I responded straining to hear her through the phone.

"My daddy gone. Good daddy. He gone!"

She repeated.

"Aw girl, he'll probably be back." I replied nonchalantly.

"Nah momma, he gone gone. The TVs gone, all his clothes, everything gone. Only thing here is our stuff!" She responded getting louder.

I couldn't believe what I was hearing. After everything we'd been through in ten and a half years. Tigga snuck out and left me without a word.

"Wow.. aight I'll be home in a few," I said to Shosh and started to figure out my exit plan from work.

I got home and sure enough, Tigga had moved out without saying a word. I felt the sting of abandonment in my chest as I looked around. I was hurt, but I never questioned it. It was at this point in my life that I was really starting to trust God, so as hurt as I was, I saw this as an opportunity for me to stop circling back to old bullshit and grow into a better person. So, after 10 and a half years together, I let him walk.

That Monday morning, barely two years into our marriage, I filed for a divorce. Our divorce took a while to be finalized. Tigga was mad that I didn't chase him. I didn't go to his job, I didn't call to ask questions, I just had him served. He kept coming up with issues for them to have to reset our court date and it just dragged the whole thing out. I was tired of chasing, tired of seeking the truth, just tired. At this point, I just wanted to build a home for Shosh and I so that I could protect her from the mess I had been through.

By the time our divorce was finalized, Shosh was 15 and starting to ask about Brick. Shosh always knew that Brick was her real father, but because Tigga was such a good dad to her, she didn't care to get to know Brick. It was Shosh who asked Tigga to be her daddy as a little girl and he happily took on that role.

I knew Shosh had to be going through her own set of emotions when she said, "Can I see my other dad now since my good daddy walked out on me?" I felt bad knowing that she didn't understand everything that was happening and was used to having a daddy in her life.

I reached out to Brick's mother to find out where he was and to let him know that his daughter was interested in getting to know him.

"Oh my God! How old is Shosh now?" Brick's mom screeched into the phone.

"15," I answered.

"You gotta bring her by the house. We haven't seen her since she was what... 4 or 5?"

I looked at Shosh. I had her grandmother on speakerphone so she was able to hear the whole conversation. Shosh gave me a quick shrug.

"OK, we'll try to come through there this weekend. Will Brick be there?" I asked. I wanted to be cordial, but I didn't want to waste my time if he wasn't going to be around either. I had to remind myself that we hadn't seen them in years and it was for good reason.

"Yea he'll be here. I'm gonna make sure he is here!" She responded.

"OK well we'll see you then," I said and got off the phone.

"You cool with going to see them too, Shosh? Your grandmother and aunty?" I asked Shoshanna.

"Yes ma, I just wanna see what he like and I guess the rest of them too. I only remember them a little bit from when I was little."

"OK. Well it's time for him to step up to the plate anyway. He ain't done shit for us in years!!" I exclaimed.

Shosh laughed, "I know! That's why we call him bad daddy!"

I felt comfortable thinking that Shosh knew what to expect with him. I didn't want her to be too disappointed if he fell off or didn't keep his word the same way Tigga did. I figured the worst he could do was let her down the way he had let me down, and I attempted to prepare her for that... Or so I thought.

That Saturday, Shosh and I pulled up to Brick's mother's house around noon. We walked up to the house slowly. It looked like very little had changed. I looked around thinking about the mess I was when I was around them back in the day. My life wasn't perfect at that moment, but it was much better than where I was back then. I had changed. I wasn't that little hood girl that lived down the street anymore. I was a business woman with goals set on having a better future than my past.

We spent the afternoon laughing and catching up with Brick, his mother, and his sister. I focused on the good memories to keep things light and comfortable for Shosh.

When we were getting ready to leave, I pulled Brick to the side. "Shoshanna wants a relationship with you. You gonna have to step up and try to be a part of her life," I stated directly.

"Yea I got you. The only reason I fell back is because I heard you was with that nigga Tig and he was trying to run shit. Otherwise I would've had you and my daughter set."

I knew he was lying right then. It's what he did. Made excuses about what he could've and should've done, then found some random scapegoat to blame for getting in his way. I wasn't even about to entertain it.

"Aight, well that nigga not around anymore, so she looking at her real daddy to step up."

"Yea. I'ma be there. Whatever she need! Y'all just let me know."

Brick's word was never as strong as Tigga, but I walked away trying to give him the benefit of the doubt. I didn't want Shosh to become overwhelmed by disappointment and abandonment the way I once was.

It wasn't long before there was an opportunity for Brick to be in Shosh's life regularly. I wanted to get Shosh thinking about her future and her career. When I was her age, my biggest concern was finding somewhere to live and making quick money to stay afloat. I couldn't really think about the future. I didn't want that for Shosh. I felt that particular parental obligation to make sure that my daughter would be set up right in life. I didn't want her to deal with the same baggage that I dealt with when I was her age. I wanted her to feel safe, loved, and courageous.

I was able to get Shoshanna an internship at the State Capitol, but I didn't have anyone to pick her up. Brick was still around the way selling drugs, so I knew he wasn't punching a clock. I saw this as a perfect opportunity for us to take him up on his offer to step up in her life and build a relationship. I figured it would be the perfect set-up for Brick to pick Shosh up at noon and either drop her off at home or go hang out with him until I got off from work. I had no clue that plan would flip my world inside out. Again.

Brick agreed to pick Shosh up from her internship in Atlanta and keep her until I got off from work. At this point, I had moved out of the home I shared with Tigga and moved into an apartment in Clarkston. Brick never wanted to drive out to Clarkston so we agreed that she would stay with him or he would drop her off at his mother's house and I would pick her up when I got off.

I agreed to let Shoshanna spend as much time with Brick as she could so that she could also get a chance to really get to know her half brother. Crazy as it was, Brick's son was the same age as Shoshanna. I knew I shouldn't have even been surprised, but my heart was once again bleeding with disgust and embarrassment. Shoshanna, being the innocent kid that she was, seemed to be very excited to meet her brother and I didn't want to steal her joy. But, the truth was, I was hurt. I hadn't been with Brick for years, yet I felt deeply for the girl I once was who loved this man so much. I realized the moment I found out about Shoshanna's half-brother, that he was never truly committed to me.

Brick kept his word and picked up Shoshanna every day. I was proud of him. I started to feel like life was falling into place again and Shosh was getting the opportunity to build a relationship with her real father.

Everything seemed to be going according to plan until I started to notice that Shosh would be so withdrawn every evening when I picked her up. She would get in the car and would barely have anything to say. When we got home, she would go straight to her room and slam the door. I knew Brick had to be around there promising her stuff and letting her down. As usual.

Tigga, her "good daddy," was a man of his word, whereas Brick was not. Brick was known for empty promises, so I wouldn't have been surprised if he was letting her down every other day. She was a teenager now, so I figured that her behavior was just a typical response to being disappointed or being told no. I never once thought that it could be anything more than that.

One Sunday afternoon, I walked into my room and noticed a letter on my bed. I turned around and Shosh was standing by the door.

"Shosh, what's this?" I asked.

"A letter," she responded timidly.

"Why you write me a letter?"

"Momma, just read it please."

"OK," I responded.

Confused by the seriousness of Shosh's tone, I sat down on the bed and picked up the letter. It was two pages. I started reading.

Dear Momma,

So, I didn't know how to tell you this and at first I wasn't going to say nothing. Every day when my daddy picks me up he tries to mess with me…

I froze. I couldn't read anymore. It was like life was instantly sucked out of me. Did my daughter just tell me that her father is molesting her? Couldn't be...

I read the sentence again hoping I was reading it wrong.

...mess with me.

I couldn't believe what I was reading. How could he disrespect our child like that? She didn't have to spell it out, nor did she have to convince me any further. I knew exactly what she was saying.

I looked up for Shosh. She had quietly walked back to her room while I was reading the letter. I knew immediately that this wasn't an easy thing for her to do. I looked back at the letter and continued reading.

My eyes welled with tears as I continued to read the details of her father's behavior. I was hurt, livid, confused. I could not let my daughter go through the same things I went through.

Since the age of 5, I had buried every unsolicited sexual encounter deep within me. I grew up subconsciously fearing the consequences of telling someone about every inappropriate sexual encounter that I had. Even while working at the funeral home in my 20s, I never once thought about saying something to somebody about what was happening with my older cousin. As I read the letter, so many emotions surfaced. But, most of all, I was proud of Shosh for having the courage to say something.

I looked up at the ceiling. "God…" I whispered with tears flowing down my face. "What do I do?"

To be continued...

ACKNOWLEDGMENTS

To all the beautiful butterflies that joined SaSumthing:

Ariona Porter, Char'Vavious Porter, Jasmine Parker, Veronica Benning, Danielle Renard, Vanessa Lomack, Phyllis Moody, Tenisha Ananaba, Venessa McCoy, Michelle Jackson, Teresa Dewberry, Yenesy Gonzalez, Destiny Heard, Katrina Correa, Sabrina Rosario, Lolita Morrison, Ashley Montaque-Drummond, Jeffrey Goodson Jr., Contressa Davis, Denise Powell, Terry Jones Jr., Khalia Franklin, Ciara Kent, Kierra Kent, Latesha Kent, Jarvis Gibson, Panya Dixon, Joani Clemons, Kimberly Varney

ACKNOWLEDGMENTS

For pushing me through:

DeKalb Rape Crisis, Yolanda,
Warren Mitchell,
Pastor Janine Howard,
Dr. Nadine C. Duncan, Antura Moore,
Coach Mustafa, David H. Pierce & Stephanie Dunford of Founders Legal,
Law & Order: Special Victims Unit

ABOUT THE AUTHOR

Awona L. Love-Thurman, also known as Summer Heat, is the founder & CEO of AnowA Foundation, Inc. --A nonprofit organization dedicated to providing support & rehabilitation for sexually abused adolescents along with adult survivors of child sexual abuse & domestic violence.

Awona is the proud grandmother of two boys. She currently resides in the Atlanta Metropolitan Area with her husband.

Visit www.sasumthing.org to learn more.

MORE BY SUMMER HEAT

A Butterfly Afraid to Fly
An Inspirational Book of Poems

CPSIA information can be obtained
at www.ICGtesting.com
Printed in the USA
BVHW030340140622
639705BV00008B/70/J